67 WAYS
TO SAVE THE ANIMALS

67 WAYS
TO SAVE THE
ANIMALS

ANNA SEQUOIA

with Animal Rights International

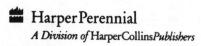

HarperPerennial

A Division of HarperCollins*Publishers*

FIRST EDITION

Designed by Barbara DuPree Knowles

LIBRARY OF CONGRESS CATALOGING-IN-PUBLICATION DATA
Sequoia, Anna.
67 ways to save the animals / Anna Sequoia with Animal Rights International.—1st ed.
    p.
  ISBN 0-06-096845-1 (pbk.)
    1. Animal welfare—United States.   2. Animal rights—United States.   I. Animal Rights International.   II. Sixty-seven ways to save the animals. III. Title.
HV4764.S47   1990
179'.3'0973—dc20   90-55185

90 91 92 93 94 CG/FG 10 9 8 7 6 5 4 3 2 1

CONTENTS

part TWO

ACKNOWLEDGMENTS

I would like to thank the following individuals and organizations from all factions of the animal rights movement who were among the many who generously shared their time, enthusiasm, concerns, research and/or advice to help create this book: African Wildlife Foundation; Alaska Wildlife Alliance; Animal Legal Defense Fund; Jonathan Boswell; California Federation for Animal Legislation; George Cave, Animal Rights Mobilization; Adele Chatelaine; Luke Dommer, The Committee to Abolish Sport Hunting; Feminists for Animal Rights; Friends of Animals; Greyhound Friends; Peter Hermance, Animal Rights Information & Education Service; The Humane Society of the United States; International Wildlife Coalition; Stephen Kaufman, M.D., Medical Research Modernization Committee; Maureen Koplow, *Animal Network Calendar of Events;* Last Chance for Animals; Bradley Miller, Humane Farming Association; Marie Moneysmith; National Alliance for Animal Legislation; New Jersey Animal Rights Alliance; New York Central Board of Education Humane Resources Committee; Brendan O'Shea; Nancy Phillips, Pure Bred Dog Rescue; Physicians Committee for Responsible Medicine; Alan Priaulx; Annemarie, Hans, Rosalie and Steve Schneider; Mark Spero, M.D.; Lynn Webb; Wildlife Refuge Reform Coalition. David Cantor, Karen Porreca and Kim Stallwood provided invaluable access to the archives of People for the Ethical Treatment of Animals; I very much appreciate their enthusiasm and support for this project. I am grateful also to Henry Spira, of Animal Rights International, for agreeing to sponsor the book.

Both *The Animals' Voice* and *The Animals' Agenda* magazines were important sources of the news that so few mainstream newspapers or magazines have seen fit to print. The term "the merchandising of extinction" was first used by Dr. Susan Lieberman of the Humane Society of the United States. The titles of chapters 3 and 8, "Puppy Mills: Puppy Hell" and "In the Name of Beauty," were first used by People for the Ethical Treatment of Animals.

Sharon O'Shea, Nancy McCarthy and Sally Lamb Bowring were good friends throughout, consistently supportive. Judd Gabey helped virtually every day. Jack London and Mabeline Sequoia, my cat friends, sat on each page. Peaches La Rue found us in time for the galleys.

I am particularly grateful to Patty Brown and John Boswell, John Boswell Associates, for helping to shape this book, and for having found the right publisher for it. Final thanks to my editor, Stephanie Gunning, and to Bill Shinker, trade division publisher, HarperCollins, for their commitment to ending animal exploitation and suffering.

PREFACE
by Henry Spira, Animal Rights International

Every day more thoughtful Americans are becoming aware of—and outraged by—the massive suffering of animals. And they want to do something about it. The most frequent question I've been asked in my sixteen years as an animal rights activist has been "What can I do to help?"

Anna Sequoia's *67 Ways to Save the Animals* is a remarkably timely and practical answer to that heartfelt question. In this one handy, easy-to-use guidebook are dozens of specific and valuable things you can do that will make a difference in areas ranging from animal agriculture to wildlife refuges. In many cases, you don't even have to leave home to be personally effective.

What you will find in these smartly organized pages are the sound tools that make rational grassroots activism work. Just two of Animal Rights International's successful campaigns may illustrate how these sensible, proven techniques made seemingly irreversible cruelty situations into key turnarounds for animal rights.

ARI's very first campaign focused on the American Museum of Natural History back in 1975, where researchers were deliberately mutilating cats to observe their sexual performance. Mass participation was crucial to the campaign's success. Hundreds of people demonstrated in front of the museum on weekends, gaining vital media attention. Others wrote and phoned museum officials, trustees, and contributors. Still others asked their legislators to contact the federal, state, and city agencies that for seventeen years had been funneling taxpayers' money toward the project. Finally, the museum was questioned and challenged on the floor of Congress. As a result of all these valid efforts, funding was stopped, the labs were dismantled, and a clear victory for animal rights was won.

Five years later, we began a public awareness campaign on the Draize rabbit-blinding test. We targeted Revlon, the cosmetics industry leader, with full-page newspaper ads asking, "How many rabbits does Revlon blind for beauty's sake?" We bought one share of Revlon stock and spoke out at shareholders' meetings. Again, we encouraged mass participation. Some activists wrote letters to the editor and reached millions with just the cost of postage stamps. (Even those letters that weren't published impressed editors with the groundswell of reader concern about the Draize test.) Others contacted radio and TV stations, favorite columnists, reporters, broadcasters, and talk-show hosts and suggested that they spotlight this mindless cruelty. The ensuing media attention and public outrage soon forced Revlon and other cosmetic companies to move toward using non-animal alternatives. By April 1990, Revlon was running full-page ads promoting their new line of skin-care products featuring a "100% non-animal-tested formula."

While emotional confrontation, self-righteousness, and demands for instant abolition may satisfy one's emotional needs, they do not really change the way animals live and die. What does promote change is becoming actively involved in activities that are practical and do-able, that focus on bite-size, step-by-step advances. Every move forward, however small, is valid on its own merits and leads to further, larger advances.

This important book takes what appears to be an overwhelming problem and with intelligence, imagination, and proven techniques, breaks it down into surmountable, bite-size pieces. I wish we had had it earlier. I'm awfully glad we have it now.

INTRODUCTION

Anyone who has ever lived with a dog or cat knows how like us they are: they enjoy their comfort, and companionship—and good meals. At times, they are deliriously happy, dogs jumping up and down with joy at the sight of us, or our friends, or other animals, cats rubbing themselves, purring, against our legs or our arms or our faces. Occasionally, our dogs and cats are bored, or anxious, or frightened. They're compassionate: they seem to sense when we don't feel well or are hurt and need comforting. They have maternal feelings, sometimes caring for puppies or kittens not their own. They experience stress. They dream. They have memories and expectations. They feel pain.

Other non-human animals are just as feeling. A chimpanzee even five years old may die of grief if something happens to his or her mother. Whales are loath to leave an injured member of their pod, often at the expense of their own safety. A pig, confined for months in the same stall as it is fattened for market, becomes chronically depressed.

In many ways, these are very cruel times, especially for animals. We are systematically cutting down the last forests that provide their shelter. We dump toxic chemicals and sewage into the waters in which they live. In Alaska, we shoot them from planes. We wear the tusks of the few remaining of their species as decorations on our arms. We gather them up in huge nets, for lunch. And each year we subject more than five billion sentient creatures to conditions of living and dying that shame us as human beings.

But this is also a time of hope. During the past decade and a half a consciousness—a conscience—about our relationship with and responsibility toward animals has risen inexorably in England, Sweden, Australia, Holland, Switzerland, Bolivia . . . and Tulsa, San Francisco, Chicago, Philadelphia, New York. It is a movement of all kinds of people, conservatives, radicals, men, women, black people, Latino people, students in high schools, students in medical schools. It is comprised of philosophers and dock workers, physicians and clerks, of people of wealth and people living on hope. The disabled have joined it and are among its most articulate spokespeople. Young people are its passionate supporters, as are the old.

The animal rights movement attracts people of good heart. It is a grass roots movement that grows each year from the soil of basic decency. It is a way of defining to ourselves who we are, as much as it is a movement to provide a better life for non-human living creatures.

This book, then, is not just about animals. It is also about us—how we can, step by step, use our tremendous power as consumers and literate citizens to eliminate one of the most entrenched bastions of injustice and suffering in our society.

Some Pragmatic Suggestions

If you don't know your congressional or senatorial district numbers, or who your representatives are, ask Information for the number of your local League of Women Voters. If you're embarrassed about not knowing, tell the volunteer you speak with at the League that you just moved to the area.

Your congressperson's address is The Honorable [his or her name], U.S. House of Representatives, Washington, DC 20515. You can contact your senators by writing to: The Honorable (his or her name), U.S. Senate, Washington, DC 20510.

If you'd like to write a few letters, but know you won't get around to it, there's a service that, for a fee of $30 a year, will compose your animal rights letters for you. Contact: The Write Cause, P.O. Box 751328, Petaluma, CA 94975, (707) 769-0116.

Join at least one animal rights organization whose work interests you. (Keep track of two or three as you go through the book.) Generally speaking, dues are very moderate. You'll receive mailings that keep you current on at least some animal rights issues—and let you know what you can do to help.

67 WAYS
TO SAVE THE ANIMALS

part ONE

"If I decide to accept your offer to buy our land, I will make one condition. The white man must treat the beasts of this land as his brothers. I am a savage and do not understand any other way. I have seen a thousand rotting buffaloes on the prairies left by the white man who shot them from a passing train. What is man without the beasts? If all the beasts were gone, men would die from great loneliness of spirit, for whatever happens to the beast also happens to the man. All things are connected. Whatever befalls the earth, befalls the sons of the earth."

—CHIEF SEATTLE

PET OVERPOPULATION:
Too Many Dogs and Cats

Chances are, if you've picked up this book, you have—or once had—a companion animal you love. That dog or cat who sleeps on your bed, or curls up next to you when you don't feel well, or makes you laugh with goofy tricks, is exceptionally lucky: he or she has a home. Millions of dogs and cats don't. Obviously, it isn't particularly comfortable to think about dogs or cats without food or shelter. But the great thing is that with a bit of thought—and not all *that* much effort, if we all work together—it's a problem we have the power to solve.

If, as you start to read, you simply don't want to confront too much reality, skip right to the solution: "What You Can Do to Help." There's also a section called "The Good News"; the simple fact is that the more of us who get involved in defending the right of every animal to lead a decent life, the more good news there is.

Background

■ There are currently 54 million companion cats in homes in the U.S., 52 million dogs, and an estimated 13 million caged birds.

■ Nevertheless, every night millions of abandoned or lost dogs and cats roam our streets looking for food.

■ One unspayed dog and her offspring can produce as many as 67,000 puppies in 6 years.

■ An unspayed female cat and her progeny can produce 420,000 kittens within 7 years.

■ Each day in the U.S., an estimated 70,000 puppies and kittens are born. Only 2 out of every 10 of these animals has a chance of finding a good home.

■ 3 out of every 7 U.S. cats are homeless.

■ Only 14 out of every 100 dogs and 9 out of every 100 cats in an animal shelter will ever find a home.

■ Anywhere from 7½ million to 20 million dogs and cats are destroyed each year, at a cost to taxpayers estimated at $250 million.

✔ **Have your dog or cat spayed or neutered.** Not spaying or neutering is no longer an option. With more than 2,500 puppies and kittens born every hour in the United States, each litter you allow to be born contributes to the millions of animals who will be euthanized in animal shelters this year, plus the millions of others in our streets who will be subjected to cruelty, starvation, disease, and death by automobile. *Please* have your animal spayed.

✔ **If you cannot afford the cost of spaying/neutering** —or if you know another animal owner in that situation—you can find the location of a low-cost program in your area by calling the Friends of Animals' spay/neuter hotline at: (800) 631-2212.

And with Just a Little More Effort You Could . . .

✔ **Volunteer to staff a hotline** during low-cost spay/neuter campaigns. To participate, call the Coalition for Pet Control at: (215) 256-0556.

✔ **Adopt an(other) animal from a shelter or veterinarian.** Every time you adopt an animal from a shelter, you save a life. Some humane veterinarians also may take in a few strays; we've had excellent luck with animals adopted via this route.

✔ **Adopt a homeless purebred dog** instead of buying one from a breeder or (*don't even think about it; we'll explain later*) a pet shop. Retired racing greyhounds, which often make fantastic, loving pets, are discussed on page 14. But you can find practically any breed that interests you. Homeless German Shepherds and Cocker Spaniels are the most readily available. There are several contacts, listed below. Tell the person you speak with which breed interests you and he or she will give you the number of someone who raises that type of dog, and who knows about possible adoptees.

Pure Bred Dog Rescue Nancy Phillips (206) 467-0205 (Seattle)	**All Breed Rescue Alliance** Kathy DeWees (609) 877-5027 (New Jersey)
Pure Bred Dog Rescue (314) 957-DOGS (St. Louis)	**All Breed Rescue Alliance** Sharon Schiele (215) 935-0896 (Pennsylvania)

If you're interested, you can also order a superb book by Shirley Weber, *Breed Rescue Efforts and Education*. It's a three-hundred-page directory of rescue organizations across the United States specializing in placing homeless purebred dogs. To order, send $15.95, plus $1.50 postage, to: Network for Animales and Females, 18707 Curry Powder Lane, Germantown, MD 20874.

✔ **Volunteer at your local animal shelter.** Many shelters need help with a variety of tasks. At Animal Aid in Tulsa, for example, one volunteer goes in every Friday to groom potential adoptees (most adoptions occur over the weekend). In New York City, the ASPCA uses volunteers to help walk dogs and socialize with both dogs and cats. Some shelters and other organizations also have outreach programs aimed at elderly people with pets: Actors and Others in North Hollywood, for example, is one of several organizations quietly providing food and veterinary assistance for fixed-income older people.

The Good News

■ The first municipal low-cost spay/neuter clinic was established in Los Angeles in 1971. Since its opening—combined with more effective public awareness programs—the number of unwanted dogs and cats euthanized in LA has dropped by more than 53 percent.

■ Santa Barbara, CA, opened a low-cost spay/neuter clinic in 1975, and has reduced the number of animals destroyed there by 80 percent.

■ The Animal Protection Institute reports that Vancouver, B.C., Canada, has had an amazing reduction of 89 percent since opening its low-cost spay/neuter clinic in 1975.

■ The Michigan Humane Society's Sterilization Program has spayed and neutered over 45,000 dogs and cats, preventing the possible birth of as many as 4.5 million excess puppies and kittens.

■ The Santa Cruz, CA, SPCA recently organized a program with eight veterinary hospitals to subsidize ten-dollar neutering operations on 200 cats. The Good Shepherd Foundation, of Nevada County, CA, offers a ten-dollar spay/neuter program to people of low income one month each year.

■ Massachusetts is now permitting elderly residents of public housing projects to keep their companion animals.

■ The First Circuit Court of Appeals has ruled that the Louisiana Board of Veterinary Medicine and Veterinary Medical Association have no right to bar the New Orleans SPCA from offering discount veterinary services.

■ Wisconsin has passed legislation making intentional animal abuse a felony.

THE ULTIMATE BETRAYAL: Pound Seizure

"The wholesale practice of pound seizure began just after World War II when the federal government began pouring vast sums of money into biomedical research. While the laboratory animal breeding industry was still in its infancy, researchers sought to acquire their experimental subjects from pounds and shelters. Pressured legislators responded with laws which required that shelter animals be made available for research, despite the fact that many physicians and scientists claimed that shelter animals' unknown genetic and environmental backgrounds made them unsuitable research models."*

Background

■ 36 states either permit or mandate that animal shelters release unclaimed companion animals to laboratories.

■ 80 percent of experiments performed on stray or former companion animals are funded by your tax dollars.

■ The laboratory research community defends pound seizure by saying that since these animals are to be "put down" anyway, it is more economical to use them than to buy dogs and cats from suppliers.

■ Laboratory researchers like to work with dogs and cats who were once companion animals because they tend to be tractable and trusting.

■ According to the Animal Protection Institute, communities that have eliminated pound seizure have found their shelters are able to place more pets and euthanize fewer because confidence in the shelter is enhanced.

3–6	Four Simple Things You Can Do to Help

✔ **Don't allow your own animals to roam about by themselves unsupervised, especially if you want to keep them out of the clutches of**

Reprinted from The Animals' Voice Magazine, P.O. Box 341347, Los Angeles, CA 90034 (800) 82-VOICE

laboratory experimenters. There are three reasons for this: first, they may get lost and wind up unidentified in a pound miles from your own community; second, they may be picked up by a "buncher" who then sells them to a laboratory; third, they could become one of the million companion animals killed each year by automobiles.

✔ **Keep identification on your animals.** Collars and I.D. tags can get lost, so many dog owners are having their dogs tattooed. Ask your veterinarian about this procedure. Or write to: National Dog Registry, Box 116, Woodstock, NY 12498, or TATTOO-A-PET, 1625 Emmons Avenue, Brooklyn, NY 11235. If you're a cat owner, you can accustom your cats to wearing collars with I.D. tags if you start when they're kittens. Do buy safety collars for your cats; these have stretchable inserts.

✔ **If you have AIDS,** and live in New York City, you can get help with dog walking, litter box cleaning, shopping for pet food, and veterinary care. You can also arrange to have your pets adopted by someone caring and kind. Contact: POWARS, Inc., P.O.Box 1116, Madison Square Station, New York, NY 10159.

✔ **Be sure there's provision in your will for your animals.** Too often well-loved companion animals wind up in pounds/laboratories because owners have no will, neglect to specify future living arrangements for their animals in their will, or simply give in to attorneys who don't think what happens to our animals is important. Be sure, too, that someone you trust has the key to your home, so that he or she can immediately provide appropriate care for your animals, should that become necessary. Give the person a signed letter from you giving your permission to take possession of your animals. You may think all this sounds paranoid, but there's reason to *be* paranoid: while researching the laboratory section of this book, we came across an account of a hideous 2-year ordeal inflicted upon a 23-year-old cat. The fact is that a cat simply doesn't get to *be* 23 years old unless it's been a well-loved pet.

And with Just a Little More Effort You Could . . .

✔ **Learn more** about pound seizure by writing to: The Humane Society of the United States, 5430 Grosvenor Lane, Suite 100, Bethesda, MD 20814, for an updated pound seizure campaign kit. EASE (Eliminate All Suffering and Exploitation), Box 5441, Santa Rosa, CA 95402, also offers a how-to packet.

✔ **If you live in San Diego County, CA,** contact: Stop Taking Our Pets, Box 1032, Solana Beach, CA 92075. They'll tell you how you can help on a local level.

✔ **Support the Pet Protection Act,** which would prohibit the National Institutes of Health, the largest financier of biomedical research in this country, from allocating any funds to researchers using lost, stolen, or shelter animals. This would effectively end 80 percent of pound seizures in the U.S. Please write to your congressional representative in care of the House of Representatives, Washington, DC 20515. Also write to your senators in care of United States Senate, Washington, DC 20510. If you do not know the names of your senators or congressional representative, or your senatorial or congressional district numbers, contact the League of Women Voters in your area.

If you'd like help drafting your letter, please feel free to copy or adapt the following:

> *The Honorable Theodore S. Weiss*
> *House of Representatives*
> *Washington, DC 20515*
>
> *Dear Congressperson Weiss:*
>
> *As a resident of the seventeenth Congressional District, and a strong believer that former companion animals should not be used in biomedical research, I am writing to urge you to reintroduce—and/or support the reintroduction of—the Pet Protection Act, which died an untimely death in the 100th Congress.*
>
> *The Pet Protection Act, as you undoubtedly recall, would prohibit any researcher who receives funding from the National Institute of Health from conducting experimentation on lost, stolen, or shelter pets. The Act would consequently end 80 percent of pound seizures in the United States.*
>
> *Respectfully,*
>
> *Anna Sequoia*

The Good News

■ 14 states have passed laws mandating that impounded dogs and cats must either be adopted out or humanely euthanized. These are Connecticut, Delaware, Hawaii, Maine, Maryland, Massachusetts, New Hampshire, New

Jersey, New York, Pennsylvania, Rhode Island, South Carolina, Vermont, West Virginia.

■ Sonoma County, CA, recently banned pound seizure.

■ Guilford County, NC, recently banned pound seizure—just a week after Duke University, the University of North Carolina, and private biomedical researchers formed an anti-animal rights alliance.

PUPPY MILLS: Puppy Hell

"Throughout the Reagan years the USDA asked for less money than it received to run its Animal and Plant Health Inspection Service, which is charged with licensing commercial breeders and brokers . . . and under the Bush Administration the service continues to have an abysmal record on regulating dog abusers."
—MARK DERR, "The Politics of Dogs," The Atlantic Monthly, March 1990

Background

■ Approximately 360,000 to 500,000 dogs sold in pet shops each year come from "puppy mills."

■ The U.S. Department of Agriculture estimates that 25 percent of the 3,500 federally licensed breeding kennels have substandard conditions.

■ As many as 1,600 kennels operating without federal licenses are never inspected.

■ The American Kennel Club, which derives millions of dollars of income each year from registration of dogs bred in puppy mills, has done virtually nothing to stop puppy mill abuses.

■ Puppy mill "breeding stock" are housed in cramped, unsanitary outdoor cages. Females are forced to breed continuously.

■ Puppy mill dogs frequently suffer from malnutrition, exposure, and genetic disorders such as hip dysplasia. Bad personality traits (i.e., biting) are perpetuated. Dogs seldom receive adequate veterinary care.

■ Puppies are taken from their mothers as early as four weeks old, and sold to brokers who pack them in crates for transport and resale to pet shops. During this shipping process, puppies frequently receive inadequate food and water.

■ Dogs from puppy mills are rarely socialized properly, causing mal-adjusted dogs that too often wind up in pounds and shelters.

■ Animals not sold before they get "too big" are killed by pet shop owners, or sold to bunchers for laboratory use. Killing methods, according to one New York City obedience trainer, most often consist of being "bashed over the head with a board."

PUPPY MILLS. Notorious breeding kennels located mostly—but not exclusively—in the Midwest, where dogs are continuously bred without regard to the animals' health, comfort, nutrition, innate personality traits, or socialization. Genetic defects are considered of no importance and passed on from generation to generation.

CATTERIES. The cat equivalent of puppy mills. Except cats are treated with even less regard.

7–8   Two Simple Things You Can Do to Help

✔ **Don't buy animals from pet shops.** There is no other more effective way of discouraging pet store owners from selling puppy mill dogs. If you'd like a particular breed of dog, with a little patience you can find a young animal of that breed at your animal shelter. Shelters frequently get golden retrievers, for example. Or contact the pure breed rescue clubs listed on page 4.

✔ **Tell your friends or relatives who may be thinking of buying a pet shop dog** about conditions in puppy mills. Show this page to them, or get a copy for them of the booklet *Pet Shops & Puppy Mills* (available from People for the Ethical Treatment of Animals, Box 42516, Washington, DC 20015).

And with Just a Little More Effort You Could . . .

✔ **Help work for desperately needed state and federal legislation.** During the 101st Congress, Congressperson Lloyd (D-TN) sponsored H.J.

Res. 57, directing the Secretary of Agriculture to conduct a study of the effectiveness of current laws and regulations in preventing inhumane treatment and premature shipment of dogs and puppies bred and raised for sale to retail pet stores. This resolution is a first step and deserves your support as well as that of your congressperson. A sample letter to a congressional representative follows. Please feel free to adapt or copy it; remember to address it to your own congressperson and to substitute your own congressional district number (call the League of Women Voters if you don't know it).

The Honorable Theodore S. Weiss
House of Representatives
Washington, DC 20515

Dear Congressperson Weiss:

I am a resident of the 17th Congressional District. I am writing to you today to urge you to co-sponsor and/or support H.J. Res. 57, which was introduced in the 101st Congress by Congressperson Lloyd (D-TN) and on which no action was taken.

H.J. Res. 57 is the first step toward creating a national policy that would adequately regulate—and, one would hope, eventually close down—puppy mills now selling half a million frequently unhealthy, abusively raised dogs to the American public via pet shops.

H.J. Res. 57 directs the Secretary of Agriculture to conduct a study of the effectiveness of current laws and regulations in preventing inhumane treatment and premature shipment of dogs and puppies bred and raised for sale to retail pet stores.

I look forward to hearing from you on this matter.

Respectfully,

Anna Sequoia

The Good News

■ In 1988, Kansas enacted a law that requires registration and semi-annual inspections of all commercial breeding kennels to ensure that dogs used for breeding have adequate shelter, food, and veterinary care.

■ Connecticut, Massachusetts, and New York have enacted legislation requiring pet stores to guarantee the health of the animals they sell. The Connecticut legislation also requires that animals in pet stores receive veterinary inspections at least every fifteen days.

THEFT OF COMPANION ANIMALS:
Safeguarding the Ones You Love

• *Each year hundreds of thousands of companion animals are stolen in the United States and Canada.*

• *Last year, the Indianapolis, IN, Lost Pet Registry reported 1,000 calls in less than one month alone.*

• *During one six-week period of the winter of 1989, 60 companion cats disappeared from Willowdale, Ontario, a vacation area north of Toronto.*

• *In cozy Lawrenceburg, IN, 9 dogs were reported missing during one week in September.*

• *Pikeville, NC, reports the sudden disappearance of 30 to 40 companion dogs.*

• *The August 20, 1989,* North Jersey Herald and News *reported "Cat-nappings on rise throughout New Jersey. Animal welfare groups in New Jersey are urging owners to safeguard family pets as the number reported missing has been on the rise in some communities . . . Humane Society of Bergen County has been receiving 5 to 6 calls a day about lost dogs or cats . . . The trend is not usual according to Action 81 . . . August and January are 'high risk' months. When family pets are missing look for signs of human involvement."*

Background

■ Anyone who wholesales 24 or more dogs per year to laboratories is supposed to be licensed by the U.S. Department of Agriculture.

■ "Class A" license dealers are invariably puppy mill and cattery operators, individuals with their own breeding operations.

■ "Class B" license dealers get their animals from "random sources." These sources usually consist of animals from shelters, "leftover" animals from pet shops, and stolen dogs. Technically, dealers are required to keep accurate records telling where all dogs were sourced—but these are frequently falsified.

■ "Class B" dealers use individuals called "bunchers"—sometimes teenagers—to obtain dogs. Bunchers have been known to use meat containing sedatives or even female dogs in heat to attract companion animals. They net cats. More deviously, they pose as humane society employees, placing stolen animals in "humane society" vans.

■ Stolen animals are transported across state lines to avoid being traced.

■ "Class B" dealers are rarely prosecuted. Those few who are prosecuted receive insignificant penalties.

Three Simple Things You Can Do to Help   9–11

✔ **Don't leave your companion animals unattended.** As inconvenient as it may at first seem, we cannot urge you too strongly not to leave your animals alone in your backyard. No free-roaming animals, of course. And if you live in a city, *please do not tie your dog to a parking meter* and then go into the supermarket or deli. A stolen dog offered for sale to a laboratory has a grim future.

✔ **Tell your friends** who leave their dogs tied to parking meters, etc., about the extent of companion animal theft. Most people simply don't know.

✔ **Don't fall prey to bunchers gathering animals to sell to laboratories.** Your "free to good home" ads that appear in the pets/classified sections of newspapers are another way bunchers gather animals. If you are offering kittens or puppies via one of these ads, at least ask to see identification (bunchers using this route generally use pseudonyms), and write down the person's license plate number.

And with Just a Little More Effort You Could . . .

✔ **Identify your local dealers.** You can get a list of licensed dealers by writing to the U.S. Department of Agriculture, Animal and Plant Health Inspection Service, Room 756, 6565 Belcrest Road, Hyattsville MD 20782. If your animals are missing, you can search dealers' premises—and do it as soon as possible—if you are accompanied by a law enforcement officer or an inspector from the APHIS.

✔ **Send for a copy** of the factsheet, " 'Pet' Theft and Animal Dealers." The hints in the sections "Targeting the Culprits" and "If the Worst Happens" are invaluable. Available from PETA, Box 42516, Washington, DC 20015-0516.

✔ **Report patterns of theft** to your local humane organization. Also to: Mary Warner, Action 81 Inc., Route 3, Box 6000, Berryville, VA 22611, (703) 955-1278. Mary Warner has become a one-person data bank of pet theft information and publishes a pet theft newsletter, *Voice of the Missing*.

✔ **Urge your congressional representative** to sponsor pet theft legislation. When you write, enclose a photocopy of the preceding pages.

GREYHOUNDS: Racing Toward Oblivion

50,000 greyhounds are born each year in breeding farms for racing. Of those, 30 percent make it to one of the 52 racetracks in the United States.

30,000 to 50,000 animals between the ages of two and five are killed, because they are not fast enough to win races.

Many of the greyhounds not fit to race are sold for research. Because of their genetic purity, they are the research model of choice for heart and lung experiments.

Greyhounds are too often trained using live bait. More than 100,000 rabbits, chickens, guinea pigs, and kittens are used each year as bait.*

Background

■ Most greyhound breeders and trainers live in the Southeast, especially Alabama, Georgia, Florida. Florida alone has more than 400 training farms.

■ Frequently, greyhounds are trained using live jackrabbits, which are attached upside down to mechanical arms that spin around the track at speeds up to 35 miles per hour. ("Baiting" greyhounds with live rabbits is a felony in Florida, but many trainers still follow this practice.)

■ To ensure that the rabbits provide a good chase but do not escape, their back legs are sometimes broken.

■ Since jackrabbits are not indigenous to the Southeast, truckloads are brought from southwestern states such as Texas and New Mexico. Often,

*Animal Protection Institute

they're not watered or fed during the trip and arrive in shock or maimed. Many do not survive the trip.

■ Following their short racing careers, greyhounds are killed, sold to laboratories for experimentation, or sent to Mexico where they are raced to the death. A few are saved each year by being adopted.

Three Simple Things You Can Do to Help | 12–14

✔ **Don't patronize greyhound racing tracks.** Ask your friends, relatives, and co-workers not to patronize greyhound races either.

✔ **To learn more,** write: Greyhound Friends, Inc., 167 Saddle Hill Road, Hopkinton, MA 01748. An upbeat video on the breed and its plight, including interviews with people who have adopted greyhounds, is available from the address above. The video will make you want a greyhound of your own.

✔ **Consider adopting a greyhound.** They're affectionate, gentle, and often make excellent pets. The phrases "most wonderful dog I've ever had" and "couch potato" come up in conversation after conversation with people who've adopted them. For information, call Louise Coleman at Greyhound Friends: (508) 435-5969. Ms. Coleman has greyhounds from eight dog tracks around New England, and has placed more than three thousand of them. Another great greyhound adoption organization is Greyhound Pets of America. They have representatives in thirty-one states. Contact: Millie Merritt, 750 Willard St., Quincy, MA 02169, (617) 472-4055.

And with Just a Little More Effort You Could . . .

✔ **Support legislative initiatives** that would require breeders and trainers to contribute toward a fund to support shelters and adoption services for retired greyhound racers.

The Good News

■ Greyhound owners and trainers are increasingly agreeing to make retired greyhounds available for adoption.

VICTIMS OF VANITY: Death by Fur Coat

"Nowhere is this indifference {to animal cruelty and exploitation} in the name of fashion more evident than in the case of fur products. Fur-bearing animals trapped in the wild inevitably suffer slow agonizing deaths. Fur farms severely limit natural movement, grooming and social behavior patterns. When we purchase the products of commercial furriers we support massive animal pain and death."

—*THE WORLD COUNCIL OF CHURCHES*

Leghold Traps

■ Each year, in the United States alone, at least 70 million animals suffer and die to produce fur garments.

■ At least 25 percent of all furs come from trapped animals.

■ An estimated 30 million animals are trapped annually in the United States.

■ 87 percent are caught using leghold traps.

■ As many as 67 percent of the animals killed in leghold traps are non-target victims. These animals include birds (including eagles), squirrels, owls, deer, dogs, cats, and endangered species. These "trash" animals are thrown out.

■ The steel jaw leghold trap is a hinged trap that slams shut on its victim's leg. The initial pain has been compared to slamming your finger in a car door. But that's not the end of it: in their terror and struggle to free themselves, animals bite at the trap, breaking teeth, as the trap tears further into their flesh, severing ligaments and breaking bone. Approximately 25 percent of trapped animals bite off their own legs to escape (trappers call this "wring off"). Animals left may remain in agony in the trap for days, only to be stomped or clubbed to death, strangled or drowned when the trapper finally returns.

■ A beaver or muskrat caught in a "drowning set"—a weighted trap deliberately set next to deep water—can take as long as 20 minutes to drown.

■ Because of its cruelty, the leghold trap is currently banned in more than fifty countries, including Switzerland, Denmark, the United Kingdom, West Germany, Chile, and Austria.

■ According to a survey conducted by Yale University, 79 percent of Americans oppose use of the leghold trap.

■ Nevertheless, in the United States, the leghold trap is banned only in Florida, Rhode Island, Hawaii, Massachusetts, and New Jersey.

■ The Department of the Interior has over 20,000 traps in use on public lands as part of "predator control" programs aimed at destruction of coyotes, mountain lions, bobcats, and other predators considered a threat by livestock ranchers using public land.

"{Lynx} kittens born in spring will usually have their pelts harvested in December, when their pelt is thick and of a fair size, but before they lose the white spotted belly that is in such high demand."

—*FUR TRADE JOURNAL OF CANADA*

ANIMAL PELTS PER COAT*

	Number of Target Animals in One 40" Coat	Number of "Trash" Animals Killed for the Coat	Hours of Agony
Coyote	16	48	960
Lynx	18	54	1080
Mink	60	180	3600
Opossum	45	135	2700
Otter	20	60	1200
Red Fox	42	126	2520
Raccoon	40	120	2400
Sable	50	150	3000
Seal	8	—	32
Muskrat	50	150	1500
Beaver	15	45	225

A Denver Wildlife Research Center study of a single coyote "control" program reported that "of 1,119 animals trapped, injured, or killed, only 138 were the targeted coyotes. The remaining victims consisted of 21 non-target species, including hawks, golden eagles, songbirds, rabbits, and deer, as well as 63 domestic animals."

—*TANJA KEOGH, Earth First!*

Courtesy of Friends of Animals

According to a handbook distributed to the German fur trade, in addition to the animals mentioned above, it takes the following quantities to create one fur coat:

130–200	chinchillas	20–30	domestic cats
40–50	martens	18–26	karakul lamb
10–12	badgers	30–45	broadtail lamb
100–400	squirrels	26–34	coypu (nutria)
18–26	fishers	12–18	ocelots
6–8	foals	60–70	skunks
120–160	hamsters	20–30	wallabies
180–240	ermines	3–5	wolves
6–10	whitecoats (seals)		

Fur "Farms"*

• *Conservative estimates are that in the United States, there are 970 mink farms, 3,000 fox farms, and 750 chinchilla farms. Other farms raise rabbits and beavers. Operations range in size from 50 + animals to thousands of animals.*

• *Foxes are kept in cages two to five feet square, with one to four animals per cage. Minks and other species are generally kept in cages one by three feet, with up to four animals per cage.*

• *Wild furbearers are by their very nature unsuited to intense confinement. Mink, for example, which account for 75 percent of the fur trade, in the wild have territorial ranges of up to 25 miles, spending 60–70 percent of their time in the water. They are by nature solitary creatures. Kept in wire mesh cages in open sheds, in hot weather they are unable, because of lack of water in which to bathe, to regulate their salivation, respiration, and body temperature. Extreme crowding also leads to self-mutilation and stereotypic, compulsive movements.*

• *Fox fare worse. In close confinement they have been known to cannibalize each other.*

• *Farm-bred wild furbearers are fed meat and fish byproducts (including entrails) unsuitable even for the pet food industry. On some ranches they are fed the bodies of other wild furbearers already skinned for their pelts.*

• *Diseases are pervasive, including severe respiratory infections, and bladder and urinary ailments. Nursing sickness is common, as are infestations of fleas, ticks, itchmites, and disease-carrying flies.*

• *Wild furbearers in captivity are not protected by the Humane Slaughter Act. Foxes' muzzles are first clamped shut, primitive electrodes are then inserted up their anuses; the current does not pass through the brain and therefore causes severe suffering during the thirty seconds to two minutes until death occurs. Other animals are killed by the poison strychnine. Still others are placed in enclosed spaces which are then filled with uncooled, unfiltered carbon monoxide from automobile exhausts; this last causes severe burning in the lungs.*

*Animal Rights Mobilization; and People for the Ethical Treatment of Animals

• *There are no federal requirements regarding humane treatment at fur farms or "ranches," and there are no inspections.*

Seven Simple Things You Can Do to Help **15–21**

✔ **Don't Buy Fur.** No coats, jackets, vests, or jackets or hats and gloves trimmed with fur.

✔ **Don't Wear Fur.** Even if it's a ten-year-old coat, by wearing it you're reinforcing the concept that wearing fur is okay; it isn't. What to do with your old fur? Give it to Goodwill or the Salvation Army. Or put it in your next yard sale and send the money you get for it to the animal rights group or animal shelter of your choice. Or send it to Animal Rights Mobilization (ARM!), or People for the Ethical Treatment of Animals, to use in one of their education programs; when you send it, tell them you'd like a receipt for tax purposes. If you'd like to send the coat to ARM! via UPS, call them first at: (717) 322-3252; in New York, you can call (212) 966-8490; in Chicago, (312) 751-0118; to call toll-free for information, (800) CALL ARM). If you'd just as soon mail it to them, the address is: P.O. Box 1553, Williamsport, PA 17703. If you'd rather send the garment to PETA via UPS, their street address is: 4980 Wyaconda Road, Rockville, MD 20852.

✔ **Talk (gently, don't be strident) to your friends and family** about not wearing fur coats or fur-trimmed garments. Some of your nouveau riche cousins will never get the message—but you'll be surprised at the number of people you can reach with gentle, informed conversation on this subject. Don't assume that your older relatives won't be receptive; we just heard a totally unexpected anti-fur statement from a relative in her late eighties.

To help convey your message, you might want to write to Friends of Animals for copies of their booklet, *The Case Against Leghold Traps*. It costs $3 for 50 copies, which you may want to distribute. Write: Friends of Animals, P.O. Box 1244, Norwalk, CT 06856.

The Humane Society of the United States has a "Shame of Fur" campaign packet, which it sells for $5 per packet: HSUS Fur Campaign, 2100 L Street, NW, Washington, DC 20037.

Animal Rights Mobilization also has excellent "Campaign for a Fur-free America" materials: when you write to them at P.O. Box 1553, Williamsport, PA 17703, to request materials, enclose a donation; they're a modestly funded grass roots organization and need the money.

People for the Ethical Treatment of Animals, P.O. Box 42516, Washington, DC 20015-0516, has a "Fur Is Dead" Action Pack available for sale;

this includes one Fur Is Dead T-shirt, a bumper sticker, a button, anti-fur cards you can use to educate fur wearers, and fact sheets and flyers. The cost is $15, including postage.

Good materials are also available from: International Wildlife Coalition (Canada), P.O. Box 461, Port Credit Postal Station, Mississauga, Ontario L5G 4M1.

✔ **Don't Buy Ekco Housewares.** The Ekco Group, Inc., the parent company of Ekco Housewares, recently purchased the Woodstream Corporation, the largest manufacturer of the leghold trap. Until Woodstream discontinues production of these cruel traps, it is important that we exercise our economic clout and not buy anything from Ekco. But just not buying isn't enough: let them know *why* you're not buying. Polite but forceful letters should be sent to: Mr. Robert Stein, President, Ekco Group, Inc., 98 Split Brook Road, Suite 102, Nashua, NH 03062. A sample letter follows:

Mr. Robert Stein
President
Ekco Group, Inc.
98 Split Brook Road, Suite 102
Nashua, New Hampshire 03062

Dear Mr. Stein:

I have been a purchaser of Ekco housewares for as long as I can remember. I particularly appreciate the fact that they are usually relatively inexpensive, and do about as good a job as more costly, "boutique" versions of the same products.

But I am writing to you now to regretfully inform you that I will no longer buy Ekco housewares—not as long as Ekco remains the owner of the Woodstream Corporation, the biggest manufacturer in the United States of the inhumane steel-jaw leghold trap.

Perhaps you are not aware that, because of its cruelty, the steel-jaw leghold trap is prohibited in more than 50 countries worldwide. Here in the United States, it was used to painfully trap approximately 26 million animals last year. As many as 67 percent of those victims were non-target animals: dogs, cats, birds, and deer.

Your decision to purchase the Woodstream Corporation was unfortunate. Your decision to retain it—and to permit it to continue production of steel-jaw leghold traps—is unconscionable.

Sincerely,

Anna Sequoia

✔ **Participate in this year's Fur Free Friday.** Scheduled for the Friday after Thanksgiving, the biggest shopping day of the year, Fur Free Friday has become an important rallying-point for anti-fur activity. It invariably gets good media attention, and helps to raise the issue of exploitation of furbearers in both the print press and on TV. If you're the shy type, you don't necessarily have to "twist and shout" to participate. In some cities, like New York, where up to a third of all fur sales take place, even your quiet presence in the line of march can have a big impact. For more information about this year's activities, contact Animal Rights Mobilization (please see the phone numbers above in "Don't Wear Fur").

✔ **Join PETA for its annual Halloween, October 31, demonstrations at Jindo fur stores** in Los Angeles, San Francisco, Miami, Atlanta, New Orleans, and other cities for a candlelight vigil to protest the beginning of the furbearer killing season at Jindo's huge Korean fur farms. For information, call: (301) 770-7444.

✔ **In Canada,** contact the Canadian Anti-Fur Alliance, a project of the Toronto Humane Society, to see what activities they have scheduled. They're at: 11 River Street, Toronto, Ontario M5A 4C2, Canada.

And with Just a Little More Effort You Could . . .

✔ **Let American Express know that you object to their featuring furs in their merchandise catalogs and bill enclosures.** Send your letters to:

Mr. Aldo Papone	**Mr. Louis Gerstner**
President	President
Travel Related Services	American Express
American Express Company	AMEX Tower
World Financial Center	200 Vesey Street
New York, NY 10285-4230	New York, NY 10285-5120

You can call them too, toll free, at: 1-800-528-8000. This may not be as effective, however, as writing the letter. Still, if you're not going to get around to writing a letter, it's better to do something . . . so call. Some animal rights activists are also cutting up their American Express cards and enclosing them with their letters.

✔ **Boycott R.H. Macy's.** Macy's has so far resisted efforts to get it to stop carrying furs. Animal Rights Mobilization is requesting that you not buy from Macy's as long as they persist in selling fur. Write to:

Mr. Herbert Wayof
President
Macy's
151 West 34 St.
New York, NY 10001

✔ **Report cases of non-target animals being caught in traps** to the Humane Society of the United States: Anti-Trapping Campaign, HSUS, 2100 L St. NW, Washington, DC 20037. This includes domestic and wild animals injured or killed in steel-jaw leghold traps, Conibear, or neck-snare traps. They'll send you a trapping case report to fill out.

A FUR GLOSSARY

PERSIAN LAMB. A lamb killed within five days of its birth, often in front of its mother.

BROADTAIL. The skin of a fetal lamb removed from its mother's womb by abortion. The abortion is induced by beating the ewe. The fetal lamb is then skinned, usually while it is still alive, to ensure the condition of its tight black curly pelt (the hair starts straightening out forty-eight hours after birth).

The Good News

■ According to a poll by *Rolling Stone* magazine, ten million Americans are now boycotting fur (four times the number who were in 1984).

■ First Lady Barbara Bush turned down the offer of an $11,000 fur coat for the Bush inauguration.

■ Soviet First Lady Raisa Gorbachev stopped wearing her furs during a visit to New York "to avoid offending Americans."

■ Trans-Species Unlimited's 1989 Fur Free Friday demonstration attracted more than 3,000 people who marched down Fifth Avenue; simultaneous demonstrations were held in ninety American cities. (Trans-Species Unlimited is now Animal Rights Mobilization.)

■ Sears Roebuck & Company no longer features fur coats in its catalog.

■ The Claridge Casino in Atlantic City cancelled a recent Mink Coat Give-A-Way after calls and letters from the New Jersey Animal Rights Alliance.

■ Actor Peter Falk has seen to it that no fur coats will be shown on his ABC TV series, *Columbo*.

■ The mail order firms F. A. O. Schwarz, Chadwick's, J. Jill, Thomas Oak, and the Tog Shop all cut furs from their catalogs.

- According to the "Fur Bearers," the wholesale fur business in Canada for the first eleven months of 1988 declined by 27 percent, from $726.9 million to $533.3 million.
- Despite well-funded opposition by the Wildlife Legislative Fund of America, the National Trappers Association, the National and State Farm Bureau Federations, and the Cattlemen's and Woolgrower's Association, residents of Nevada County, California, voted overwhelmingly to abolish the manufacture, sale, or use of leghold traps.
- Designer Bill Blass will no longer design fur coats. Nor will Carolina Herrera, Oleg Cassini, and Norma Kamali.
- 1989 Miss Universe, Angela Visser of the Netherlands, refused to accept a gift of fur.
- The Franklin Mint agreed to stop trimming its dolls in real fur after briefly being the target of a letter-writing and call-in campaign.
- Designer Giorgio Armani recently decorated the linings of his faux fur coats with an animal rights statement.
- As reported in *The Animals' Voice* magazine, "Los Angeles County Agricultural Commissioner E. Leon Spaugy ordered LA county trappers to stop using the steel-jawed leghold traps after county residents, responding to a report that a coyote in Topanga Canyon chewed off its leg to escape from a trap, complained about the cruelty of the device to county supervisors."
- Business was so bad during 1989 that the Montreal Fur Baron's Ball was cancelled due to poor ticket sales.
- The annual New York Fur Expo scheduled for May of 1989 was cancelled because of lack of exhibitor interest.

"Possibly the most damaging in terms of the overall market picture is the situation in Europe. For all practical purposes we have lost Western Europe. Generally considered the major world market for our wild furs, the European market fell in less than three years from the top consuming region to an area where furs are now looked upon with distaste."

—PARKER L. DOZHIER,
The Trapper and Predator Caller

Fur Wearers Hall of Shame*

The following high-profile individuals and organizations continue to wear, design, or promote fur.

*Reprinted courtesy of People for the Ethical Treatment of Animals.

Adolfo
American Express
Roseanne Barr
Bloomingdale's
Suzy Chaffee
Oscar de la Renta
Diner's Club
E. L. Doctorow (recently seen wearing a wolf-trimmed parka)

Gian Franco Ferre
Leona Helmsley
Donna Karan
Calvin Klein
Ann Landers
Bob Mackie
Macy's
Claude Montana
Neiman-Marcus
Yves St. Laurent

Leonard Nimoy (another wolf-trimmed parka)
Jackie Onassis
Nancy Reagan
Barbra Streisand
Elizabeth Taylor
Steve Thomas ("This Old House" host)
Oprah Winfrey
Vogue

Some Celebrities Who Won't Wear Fur

Richard Adams
Ann-Margret
Dan Aykroyd
Joan Baez
Kevin Bacon
Brigitte Bardot
Bob Barker
Kim Bassinger
Candice Bergen
Timothy Bottoms
Christie Brinkley
Morgan Brittany
Carol Burnett
Belinda Carlisle
Julie Christie
Jamie Lee Curtis
Doris Day
Bo Derek
Diana, Princess of Wales
Angie Dickinson
Clint Eastwood
Federico Fellini
Roberta Flack
John Forsyth
Zsa Zsa Gabor
Peter Gabriel
Jane Goodall
Daryl Hannah
Tippi Hedren

Earl Holliman
Michael Jackson
Van Johnson
Jack Jones
Ben Kingsley
Lorenzo Lamas
Jack Lemmon
Ira Levin
Art Linkletter
Joanna Lumley
Ali MacGraw
Steve Martin
Marsha Mason
Linda McCartney
Paul McCartney
Rue McClanahan
Sandy McCormack
Virginia McKenna
Yehudi Menuhin
Burgess Meredith
Yvette Mimieux
Liza Minelli
Dudley Moore
Spike Mulligan
Rita Moreno
Paul Newman
Olivia Newton-John
Kim Novak
Carrie Otis

Floyd Patterson
Cassandra "Elvira" Peterson
River Phoenix
Diana Ross
Ringo Starr
James Stewart
Sting
Peter Strauss
Sally Struthers
Loretta Swit
Rod Taylor
Toni Tenille
The Aga Khan
Lily Tomlin
Daniel J. Travanti
Bill Travers
Twiggy
Brenda Vaccaro
Alice Walker
Dennis Weaver
Jane Weidlin
Betty White
Veronica Wilson
Gretchen Wyler
Jane Wyman
Susannah York
Loretta Young
Stephanie Zimbalist

THOSE CUTE BABY HARP SEALS:
The Scandal Is That They're Still Being Killed

In 1985, most of us were more than slightly relieved to hear that the infamous baby Harp seal hunt of Atlantic Canada was over. *No one* wanted to have to look again, even briefly, at those pictures ... those scenes of appealing, dark-eyed, puppy-like creatures being clubbed to death and bleeding on the ice.

Unfortunately, there is mind-boggling news: *Canadian sealers and fishermen have revived the Harp seal hunt.*

Background

■ Baby Harp seals are born with the soft white coat we've all seen in those news clips.

■ At the age of ten days, baby Harp seals begin to molt. Their fur gradually turns a silvery gray.

■ The Canadian Ministry of Fisheries and Oceans had announced that newborn (whitecoat) baby Harp seals would no longer be hunted for "commercial" purposes. They neglected to say anything about the ten-days-to-one-month-old graycoated baby seals.

■ In 1988, more than 80,000 graycoated Harp seal pups were slaughtered; in 1989, 66,175 were killed.

■ The younger—ten-days- to two-week-old seals—were clubbed to death. Slightly older seals were shot.

■ Shooting from small boats in choppy waters, hunters kill or wound many more Harp seal pups than they recover; it has been estimated that as many as two-thirds sink under water.

Two Simple Things You Can Do to Help   **22–23**

✔ **Write to Tom Siddon, Minister of Fisheries and Oceans,** Canadian Department of Fisheries and Oceans, 200 Kent Street, Ottawa, Ontario,

Canada K1A oE6. Tell him that you are outraged by the slaughter of thousands of seal pups.

✔ **If you can afford it, consider participating in a Seal Watch trip.** These are annual events, sponsored by the International Fund for Animal Welfare (please see page 118 for more specifics about the trip). They sound like a lot of fun, and the hope is that ultimately they'll make tourism more profitable for the local population than the graycoat seal hunt that occurs right after the American tourists leave.

WHY IT'S STILL GOING ON

The Canadian government allocated $5,000,000 to "revitalize" the small boat commercial hunt.

The European fur industry is still using seal pelts and seal leather.

There is an ever-growing Asian market for aphrodisiacs. In this case, it's a powder made from baby seal penis bones, testicles, and toes.

Tons of processed seal meat and seal oil are now being fed to "ranch"-raised mink and fox.

A Canadian food processing company has begun development of microwaveable seal tidbits for humans: "breaded seal nuggets, pepperoni seal sausages, frozen flipper pie." (Reported in *The Sunday Express,* St. Johns, Newfoundland; courtesy of the International Wildlife Coalition.)

IN THE NAME OF BEAUTY:
The Hidden Cruelty of Cosmetics and Personal Care Products

■ Americans spend approximately $18.5 billion a year on cosmetics and personal care products. Every week, more than one hundred new products of this type are released into the market.

■ Two of the four U.S. cosmetics companies doing the largest dollar volume of business annually*—Revlon and Avon—have (at least for the

Figures reported for 1988

moment) stopped testing their products on animals. More than 220 cosmetics and household product companies now profitably use non-animal testing methods.

■ In the cosmetics industry, cruelty-free products are one of the fastest-growing market segments. One distributor, Body Shop, Inc., has expanded from a single store fourteen years ago to more than 350 today.

■ No law requires that cosmetics or household products be tested on animals. Nevertheless, by six o'clock this evening, hundreds of animals will have had their eyes, skin, or gastrointestinal systems unnecessarily burned or destroyed. Many animals will suffer and die this year to produce "new" versions of deodorant, hairspray, lipstick, and nail polish.

■ The Cosmetic, Toiletry and Fragrance Association is in the process of raising $1,000,000—not to find alternatives to animal testing, but rather to fight animal rights activists.

The Draize Test

■ The Draize Acute Eye-Irritancy Test was developed more than 50 years ago by Dr. John Draize, of the U.S. Food and Drug Administration, as a means of screening substances being considered for chemical warfare. In 1944, it was adopted in this country as the standard test for eye irritancy.

■ The Draize test is performed almost exclusively on albino rabbits. These are the preferred subjects because they are docile, cheap, and their eyes do not shed tears (so chemicals placed in them don't wash out). They are also the test subject of choice because their eyes are clear, making it easy to observe destruction of eye tissue; their thin corneal membranes are extremely susceptible to injury.

■ During each Draize test, 6 to 18 rabbits are immobilized (usually in a "stock," with only their heads protruding)—and a solid or liquid is placed in the lower lid of one eye of each rabbit. These substances can range from mascara to aftershave lotion to oven cleaner. The rabbits' eyes remain clipped open. Anaesthesia is rarely administered.

■ Rabbits are then examined at intervals of 1, 24, 48, 72, and 168 hours. Reactions, which may range from severe inflammation, to clouding of the cornea, to ulceration and rupture of the eyeball, are recorded by technicians. Some studies continue for a period of weeks. No attempt is made to treat the rabbits or to seek antidotes.

■ Rabbits who survive the Draize test may then be used as subjects for skin-irritancy tests.

What's Wrong with the Draize Test

■ Rabbits' eyes are not the same as human eyes; there are profound differences between them. Substances that fail to damage rabbits' eyes may in fact be toxic to humans.

■ The Draize test is essentially a "pass/fail" test. It may indicate that a substance is irritating—but not *how* irritating.

■ Test results are difficult to reproduce. Reporting depends upon subjective judgments made by laboratory personnel. Results vary from laboratory to laboratory.

■ Products that have been proven to be irritants are still being sold.

■ When a product does get into someone's eye, the treatment is not based on Draize data.

■ It's cruelty.

The Good News: There Are Now Alternatives to the Draize Test

The EYTEX System. The EYTEX System was developed by the National Testing Corporation and is now being used to determine eye irritancy of substances as diverse as toothpaste and paint. The system is rapid, easy to perform, objective, reproducible and inexpensive (90 percent cheaper than the Draize test). EYTEX is currently in use by many research and development firms.

The Agarose Diffusion Method. As reported by Neal D. Barnard, M.D., chairman of the Physicians Committee for Responsible Medicine, in *Animals' Agenda* magazine, "the agarose method has long been used for testing the safety of plastics and other synthetic materials in medical devices that come in contact with human tissues. Heart valves, intravenous lines, artificial joints, and other products have been tested for irritancy with this method for about 25 years." Adapted for use on cosmetics, this new method costs $50 to $100 per product compared to $500 to $700 per product for the Draize. The test can be run in twenty-four hours, much more quickly than the Draize, and it can be run in any microbiology laboratory with uniform results. "The test uses cells that originally came from mice. However, these cells are now obtained from cultured immortal cell lines, so no further animals are required."

Acute Toxicity Tests:
The Infamous LD50

LD50 is the abbreviation of Lethal Dose 50—the lethal dose that will kill 50 percent of all animals in a test group of 40 to 200 animals.

Most commonly, animals are force-fed substances (which may be toothpaste, shaving cream, drain cleaner, or pesticides) through a stomach tube and observed for two weeks, or until death. Non-oral methods of administering the test include injection, forced inhalation, or application directly to an animal's skin (including application to the animal's rectum or vagina).

Symptoms routinely include tremors, convulsions, vomiting, diarrhea, paralysis, or bleeding from the eyes, nose, mouth. Animals who survive the test are destroyed.

The LD50 test, which has been used for more than sixty years in twenty countries, mostly uses rodents—but the test has also frequently been performed on dogs and cats.

The federal government no longer requires the LD50 test to verify a product's safety.

What's Wrong with the LD50 Test:
Scientists Speak Out

"{The LD50 is} a ritual mass execution of animals ... a wasteful endeavor in which scientific inventiveness and common sense have been replaced by a thoughtless completion of senseless protocols.... Clinical experience shows that the LD50 value determined in animals rarely bears a meaningful relation with the lethal dose in man."
    —DR. GERHARD ZBINDEN, University of Zurich, Consulting toxicologist to the World Health Organization

"... an anachronism.... I do not think the LD50 test provides much useful information about the health hazards to humans from chemicals...."
                —DR. DAVID P. RALL, Director, National Toxicology Program

"Routine use of the quantitative LD50 is not now scientifically justified ..."
                —NATIONAL SOCIETY FOR MEDICAL RESEARCH

24–29 Six Simple Things You Can Do to Help

✔ **Buy cosmetics, personal care, and household products that have not been tested on animals.** You'll have *lots* from which to choose . . . On the pages that follow, you'll find a list of brands not tested on animals, including a separate list of very familiar brands like Nexxus, Revlon, Almay, and more. We'll tell you where you can get a wallet-sized version of the list, so you can carry it with you when you shop. And we've also provided, on page 95, a guide to cruelty-free shopping by mail—a guide that includes some surprising cruelty-free products, like paint and floor wax, as well as shampoo, mascara, and home permanents. The products in that guide have been evaluated for price, too, and you'll find some real bargains in everything from night creams to wool wash and detergent. And there's a bonus, too: virtually without exception, every household product mentioned is also non-polluting and safe for the environment.

✔ **Encourage your friends, family, and co-workers to buy cruelty-free** cosmetics, personal care, and household products too. You'd be surprised at how much influence you have. If you need "back-up," encourage the people you speak with to read the parts of this chapter on Draize and LD50 testing.

✔ **Instead of buying all your personal care and household products, why not make some yourself?** It's simple, inexpensive, kind to animals, ecologically sound. On page 106, we'll show you how.

✔ **Please boycott all products produced by Gillette until they stop testing on animals.** You'll be surprised by some of these products: Liquid Paper Correction Fluid; PaperMate pens; Flair pens; S. T. Dupont pens; Trac II and Daisy razors. Other, perhaps more obvious Gillette products are Dry Idea, Right Guard, Imagine Body Spray, Soft & Dry deodorants; Mink Difference, Tame, Toni Home Permanents, Silkience, The Dry Look, and White Rain hair care products; Face Saver, Good News and Gillette Swivel razors and blades; Oral B toothbrushes.

Here's the story: despite Gillette's letters to consumers stating that they had long since stopped performing the LD50 and other painful and/or fatal tests on animals, an employee of their Rockville, Maryland, laboratory in 1985 documented—in still photographs and on videotape—the fact that Gillette continued, for example, to test dandruff shampoo on rabbits until their skin blistered and peeled, and killed rats by forcing them to inhale massive amounts of hairspray and aerosol deodorants. For a variety of reasons, including pressure from animal rights groups, that laboratory was soon closed, but the very same tests were farmed out to other laboratories where they still go on. Gillette's resistance to establishing humane testing procedures is, in our opinion, nothing short of stubborn for stubbornness' sake—and at this point, only pressure from consumers can help remedy the situation.

For more information about the Gillette boycott, you can contact its sponsor: ARK II, P.O. Box 11049, Washington, DC 20008, (301) 897-5429; or ARK II, 542 Mount Pleasant Road, Suite 104, Toronto, Ontario M4S 2M7, (416) 487-4681. This boycott is also receiving strong support from PETA and the National Anti-Vivisection Society.

To express your dissatisfaction with Gillette's policies, please write to:

Mr. Colman Mockler
Chief Executive Officer
The Gillette Company
Prudential Tower Building
Boston, MA 02199
(617) 421-7000

Mr. Ronald J. Rossi
President
Gillette Canada
5450 Cote de Liesse Road
Montreal, Quebec H4P 1A7

Please send copies of any replies to ARK II.

✔ **If you formerly bought products from a cosmetics company that tests on animals,** let them know why you won't be buying from them any more. If you live in the New York City area, where so many major cosmetics manufacturers have corporate offices—or if you don't mind the cost of a long-distance call—the easiest thing to do is to call. Ask to speak with the director of public relations. Obviously, these people are adept at deflecting criticism, but we know from our own experience inside a corporation that these calls can make a difference if there are enough of them. The first call may make you feel awkward; that's normal. But you'll be surprised at how good it makes you feel, too. By the time you make your second call, you'll be an expert animal activist. Just be calm, polite, and tell them why you won't be buying their product any more until they stop testing on animals.

If you prefer to write to a company whose product you formerly bought, a sample letter follows. Please feel free to copy as much of it as you wish or to adapt it to your own experience.

Mr. Ari Kopelman
President
Chanel, Inc.
9 West 57 Street
New York, New York 10019

Dear Mr. Kopelman:

While preparing my income tax, I came across receipts for Chanel cosmetics I had charged during the past year. You may be interested in the fact that I spent well over $200 on your products within the past twelve months . . . and that I will not again purchase Chanel colognes or cosmetics until your company stops doing testing on animals.

As you are undoubtedly aware, Revlon no longer tests on animals. Nor do Almay, Avon, Charles of the Ritz, Christian Dior, Germaine Monteil. Given the state of current technology, specifically the EYTEX System and the Agarose Diffusion Method tests, the Draize skin irritancy and LD50 tests you now perform on animals are unnecessary—and inhumane. They're also costing you money in lost sales.

I sincerely hope that Chanel will very soon end all testing on animals. Times are changing. Your market has changed. Even your formerly most loyal customers now purchase only cruelty-free cosmetics.

Sincerely,

Anna Sequoia

✔ **Don't forget to call or write companies which have stopped doing animal testing!** If you've just switched to Charles of the Ritz cosmetics, say, from another company that tested on animals, let them know. There's always the danger that companies will go back to animal testing—so the fact that they're attracting clientele by *not* testing is an important sales factor.

Here are just a few people you may want to thank:

Mr. Ronald O. Perleman	**Mr. James Preston**	**Mr. Jay Van Andel**
President, Revlon	Chairman, Avon	Chairman of the Board
625 Madison Avenue	9 West 57 Street	Amway Corporation
New York, NY 10022	New York, NY 10019	7575 East Fulton Road
(212) 527-4000	(212) 546-6015	Ada, MI 49355
		(616) 676-6000

And with Just a Little More Effort You Could . . .

✔ **Are you interested in buying stock, but want it to be in corporations that do not test on animals?** Prudential-Bache Securities has begun to offer specially-tailored investments for the humane and animal rights community. Contact: Robert Tonnesen, Jr., (800) 356-6917, or write to him at: 153 Main Street, Hackettstown, NJ 07840. Fax: (201) 850-5439.

✔ **Urge your legislators to support H.R. 1676, the Consumer Products Safe Testing Act.** Introduced by Barbara Boxer (D-CA), H.R. 1676 would prohibit using the LD50 test for product safety, labeling, and transportation requirements. It also requires federal agencies to review other animal toxicity tests and come up with regulations to replace them if valid alternatives exist. At last count, this bill has 106 cosponsors; it's time for some action on it. Your letters could make a real difference.

✔ **Do you own stock in a corporation that is still testing on animals?** Stockholders can have tremendous impact if they band together. In the past three years alone, the number of stockholder resolutions introduced on the matter of product testing on animals has grown substantially. If you do own stock and would like to help use it to end animal testing, contact: Susan Rich, Compassion Campaign Coordinator, PETA, at: (301) 770-7444.

✔ **If you are a resident of Illinois.** The Illinois Citizens for Humane Legislation is working on stopping the Draize and skin irritancy tests in your state. To offer your help, call: (312) 288-3838. For more information, send a SASE to 2520 N. Lincoln Ave., Box 170, Chicago, IL 60614.

PETA's Cruelty-Free Shopping Guide*

Cruelty-free products are produced *without* animal testing and *without* animal ingredients. The following companies distribute products—primarily household products, cosmetics, and personal care items—that are cruelty-free:

Abracadabra	American Merfluan
Aditi Nutrisentials	Ananda Country Products
AFM Enterprises	Aroma Vera Co.
Allens Naturally	Aura Cacia

Reprinted courtesy of People for the Ethical Treatment of Animals

Auromere Ayurvedic Imports
Avanza
Aztec Secret
Baby Touch
Baubiologie Hardware
Biogime International
Body Love
Bug-Off
Cernitin America
Clearly Natural Products
Color Quest
Comfort Mfg. Co.
Dr. E. H. Bronner
Duncan Enterprises
Forever New
Granny's Old-Fashioned
   Products
Home Services Products Co.
Huish Chemical Co.
Integrated Health

International Rotex
LaCrista
Martin Von Myering
Mia Rose Products
Microbalanced Products
Mountain Fresh Products
New Age Products
Neway
No Common Scents
Paul Penders USA
Pets 'N People
Sappo Hill Soapworks
Shahin Soap Co.
Simplers Botanical Co.
Sirena Tropical Soap Co.
Soap Factory
Warm Earth Cosmetics
Without Harm
Youthessence

Many other products are *not* tested on animals, but *may contain animal-derived ingredients* including milk and egg byproducts or lanolin from sheep. Please check labels for product ingredients to determine the exact contents. The following companies distribute products that are not tested on animals, but which may contain animal ingredients:

A Clear Alternative
ABEnterprises
Advanced Design Laboratories
African Bio-Botanica
Alba Botanica Cosmetics
Alexandra Avery Purely Natural
Alexandra de Markoff
Almay
Alvin Last
Amberwood
Amway
Andalina
Arbonne International
Ardell International
Armstrong World Industries
Atta Lavi

Aubrey Organics
Auroma International
Austin Diversified Products
Autumn-Harp
Aveda Corporation
Avon
Ayagutaq
Barbizon International
Bare Escentuals
Basically Natural
Bath Institute
Baudelaire
Beauty Naturally
Beauty Without Cruelty
   (Pamela Marsen)
Beehive Botanicals

Bennetton Cosmetics Corp.
Biokosma
Bo-Chem Co.
Body Shop
Boerlind of Germany
Bonne Sante
Botanicus Retail
Breezy Balms
Bronson Pharmaceuticals
C. W. Bodkins
Carlson Labs
Carma Laboratories
Carole's Cosmetics
Caswell-Massey
Charles of the Ritz
Chempoint Products
Chenti Products
Christian Dior Perfumes
Clientele
Columbia Cosmetics Mfg.
Come to Your Senses
Compassionate Consumer
Compassion Cosmetics
Country Comfort
Crabtree & Evelyn
Creature Comfort
Creighton's Naturally
Critter Comfort
Cruelty-Free Cosmetics Plus
DeLore International
Dermatone Laboratories
Desert Essence
Dr. Babor Natural Cosmetics
Dr. Hauschka Cosmetics
Earth Science
Ecco Bella
EcoSafe Laboratories
Ecover
Elizabeth Grady Face First
Espree Cosmetics
EvaJon Cosmetics
Everybody

Farmavita USA
Finelle Cosmetics
Fleur de Santé
Flora Distributors
Focus 21 International
Freeman Cosmetic Corp.
G. T. International
General Nutrition
Germaine Monteil
Giorgio
Giovanni Cosmetics
Glowing Touch
Golden Lotus
Golden Pride/Rawleigh
Grace Cosmetics
Gruene
Heart's Desire
Heavenly Soap
Helen Lee
Hewitt
Home Health Products
Houbigant
Humane Alternative Products
Humphreys Pharmaceutical
Ida Grae Products
Image Laboratories
i Natural
Institute of Trichology
International Vitamin Corp.
InterNatural
Isadora
Jacki's Magic Lotion
James Austin Company
Jason Natural Products
Jean Naté
Jeanne Gatineau
Jeanne Rose Herbal Body Works
Jean-Pierre Sand
John F. Amico & Co.
John Paul Mitchell Systems
JOICO Laboratories
Jurlique Cosmetics

Kallima
Kenra Laboratories
Kimberly Sayer
Kiss My Face
Kleen Brite Laboratories
KMS Research
KSA Jojoba
L'anza Research Laboratories
Levlad
Life Start Healthways
Life Tree Products
Lily of Colorado
Lily of the Desert
Lion & Lamb
Livos Plant Chemistry
Lotus Light
Lowenkamp International
Luseaux Laboratories
Luzier Personalized Cosmetics
Magic of Aloe
Marie Lacoste Enterprises
Martha Hill Cosmetics
Matrix Essentials
Max Factor
McGean-Rohco
Metrin Laboratories
MFM Industries
Michael's Health Products
Mira Linder Spa in the City
Mountain Ocean
Naturade Cosmetics
Natural Organics
Nature Basics
Nature Cosmetics
Nature de France
Nature's Gate Herbal Cosmetics
Nature's Plus
Nectarine
New Age Creations/Herbal
  Bodyworks
Nexxus
North Country Soap

NuSkin
Nu Sun
Nutri-Metrics International
Oriental Beauty Secrets
Orjene Natural Cosmetics
Oxy Fresh
P. Leiner Nutritional Products
  Corp.
Painlessly Beautiful
Parfums Givenchy
Patricia Allison
Paul Mazzotta
Paul Penders USA
PetGuard
Phoenix Laboratories Interna-
  tional
Prestige Fragrances
Princess Marcella Borghese
Pro-Line
Pro-Ma Systems
Puritan's Pride
Queen Helene
Rachel Perry
Rainbow Concepts
Rainbow Research Corp.
Redken Laboratories
Red Saffron
Reviva Labs
Revlon
Roc
Royal Laboratories
RR Industries
Rusk
Scarborough & Co.
Sebastian International
Shaklee
Shikai Products
Shirley Price Aromatherapy
Sierra Dawn
Sombra Cosmetics
Sorik International
Spare the Animals

Sparkle Glass Cleaner
St. Ives
Studio Magic
Sukesha
Sunrise Lane Products
Sunshine Products Group
TerraNova
Tom's of Maine
Tonialg Cosmetics International
Truly Moist
Tyra Skin Care
Ultima II
Ultra Beauty
Val-Chem

Velvet Products Co.
Victoria Jackson
Visage Beauté
Viviane Woodward Cosmetics
Wachter's Organic Sea Products
Watkins
Weleda
Wise Ways Herbals
Wite-Out
Wysong Corporation
Yves Rocher
Zia Cosmetics
Zinzaré

Companies listed have given PETA a signed Statement of Assurance or a letter stating their position on animal testing. Some companies may be cruelty-free but if they have not sent PETA a letter or Statement of Assurance they are not included. This list is based on the most current information at the time of printing; please call to verify the status of unlisted companies (301-770-7444). PETA states that it reserves the right to choose which companies will be included, based on company policy.

To obtain a wallet-sized copy of the preceding list, send a self-addressed, stamped envelope with your request for the *PETA Cruelty-Free Shopping Guide* to PETA, P.O. Box 42516, Washington, DC 20015.

Another source of information on shopping with a conscience is the Council on Economic Priorities. Their book, *Shopping for a Better World: A Quick & Easy Guide to Socially Responsible Supermarket Shopping* (Ballantine Books, $4.95) rates 168 companies and 1,800 products on a variety of social concerns, including animal testing. If you buy it, be sure to read carefully the key to the symbols used (companies with checks with a star next to them indicate that a company is still doing animal testing, but at a reduced level, and/or has given $250,000 or more to research in alternatives; you'll have to make up your mind for yourself whether you want to buy from companies doing any testing on animals at all). The Council on Economic Priorities will also soon publish *Investing in America's Corporate Conscience* (Prentice Hall), which will compare "ethical" companies with Fortune 500 companies.

A shopping reminder: Carmé, long a favorite of humane shoppers, recently sold 49 percent of their stock to a company that does extensive animal testing. Therefore, you'll undoubtedly want to avoid the brands they manufacture: Carmé, Loanda, Mild and Natural, Mill Creek, Mountain Herbery, and Sleepy Hollow Botanicals.

HUNTING: What's Wrong with It, Anyway?

"The sports-hunting Establishment—the numerous private and public agencies, industries and lobbies whose life depends upon the killing of our native fauna for pleasure—is the most pampered, privileged, subsidized recreational group in existence. Nevertheless, it has a paranoiac fear of even the mildest criticism."

—BIL GILBERT, Saturday Evening Post

The Annual Kill

• *More than 175 million animals are killed by hunters in the United States yearly.*

• *For every animal killed, two are seriously injured and left to die a slow death.*

• *According to Wayne Pacelle, executive director of the Fund for Animals, writing in* Animals' Agenda, *in 1987 hunters killed and crippled 10 million ducks (whose numbers are now at dangerously low levels).*

• *Luke A. Dommer, president of the Committee to Abolish Sport Hunting, estimates the annual kill by hunters as 21 million waterfowl, 3 million deer, 27 million rabbits, 32 million squirrels, 91 million upland birds, and over 225,000 bears, caribou, moose, and antelope.*

- *Each year, hunters kill an average of 400 people.*
- *The toll in fear and suffering cannot be quantified.*

Lead Shot

■ All it takes is one lead shotgun pellet, mistaken for a pebble, to poison a waterfowl.

■ Lead shot from shotguns kills 3 million waterfowl a year through ingestion alone.

■ Lead shot has been building up in our wetlands at approximately 6,000 tons—30 billion pellets—a year.

■ Even though lead shot will be banned in 1991, the millions of pounds already left in our wetlands by hunters will poison waterfowl, carrion-eating birds, and natural predators for decades to come.

How Many Hunters Are There, and Why Do They Kill?

There are nearly 21.5 million hunters in the United States. Approximately 5 million of them hunt without licenses.

The late Dr. Karl Menninger, Sr., ascribed hunters' "joy of killing or inflicting pain" to having "erotic sadistic motivation." Most hunters say they like the fresh air, exercise, and—can you believe it?—being so close to nature.

Unexpected Supporters of Hunting

Some of the "conservation" or "wildlife" organizations below issue statements about the rights of subsistence hunters, some talk about controlling wildlife expanding beyond reserves and parks, and some won't address the issue at all. Before adding any further to their coffers, ask them if they have a copy of their position on the issue and make up your mind for yourself.

American Forestry Association	Isaak Walton League
American Wildlife Institute	National Audubon Society*
Ducks Unlimited, Inc.	National Wildlife Federation
Game Conservation International	The Sierra Club**

*While the Audubon Society claims to be neutral on the subject of hunting, in the past it has supported sport hunting of mourning doves, woodcocks, white-winged and white-tipped doves.

**The Sierra Club stated to us that it has "no official policy on hunting or trapping." Nor did they wish to make one. The fact that they have this long refused to make an anti-hunting statement is interpreted by some in the animal rights movement as complicity with the hunting lobby and the Department of the Interior, in exchange for funding from the former and favored treatment from the latter.

The Wilderness Society
The Wildlife Society
Wildlife Legislative Fund
Wildlife Management Institute

World Wildlife Fund
(World Wide Fund for Animals)

30–31   Two Simple Things You Can Do to Help

✔ **Before contributing to a "wildlife" group,** ask if it supports hunting. Specifically, you may want to ask for its position on sport hunting.

✔ **Post "No Hunting" signs on your land,** even if you have a wooded acre-and-a-half in suburbia.

599,526 acres were flooded to attract migrating geese and ducks for the hunters' guns.

32,640 miles of roads were constructed in the wilderness to give hunters better access for the killing of wildlife.

(The above data are for 1975. It has continued annually at an increasing rate.)

The Fish and Wildlife Service's (FWS) and State Game Commissions' "controlled burns" and "prescribed fires" frequently get out of control. One example: in 1976 the FWS told the State of Michigan to "let burn" a quarter-acre fire in order to "promote vegetative conditions favoring wildlife production." Before the fire was contained (at a cost of over $3 million to the federal taxpayer) 70,000 acres of the Seney National Wildlife Refuge and the Manistique River Forest were burned. No estimate of the number of animals roasted to death was presented at congressional hearings.

Millions of wild creatures are burned, mangled, or drowned during such "habitat manipulation." Species that require old forest or meadowland for survival lose their habitat permanently—and become extinct.

"Habitat manipulation," hunting, and trapping are permitted on about 700 million acres of public land. These activities then bar from the land the 93 percent of Americans who do not hunt or trap.

The Supreme Court of the United States held, in 1842, that wildlife is held in trust for *all* the people.

And with Just a Little More Effort You Could . . .

✔ **Ostracize hunters and trappers.** Don't buy from their stores and don't patronize their services.

✔ **Ask your legislators** to work for reorganization of the U.S. Department of the Interior's Fish and Wildlife Service and State Game Commissions so that all animals, *including* "game" animals, are protected.

✔ **Demand an end to hunting and trapping** on all public land.

✔ **Buy paper company or timber corporation stock together with other animal rights friends.** Submit a proposal that hunting and trapping be banned from all forests owned by the company.

TROUBLE IN PARADISE:
The National Wildlife Refuge System

■ There are currently 442 refuges in the National Wildlife Refuge System, or approximately 88½ million acres. These range from the Arctic to the Florida Keys, from Maine to American Samoa.

■ Hunting is permitted on 259 of our National Wildlife Refuges.

■ Trapping—including trapping for commercial purposes (i.e, fur coats)—is permitted on 91.

■ Fifty-five of those refuges encourage trapping as a "management tool"; these traps are tended by federal employees whose salary you pay.

"The real cure for our environmental problems is to understand that our job is to salvage Mother Nature . . . We are facing a formidable enemy in this field. It is the hunters . . . and to convince them to leave their guns on the wall is going to be very difficult . . ."

—JACQUES COUSTEAU

Background

■ The National Wildlife Refuge System was established in 1903 by Theodore Roosevelt to provide "inviolate sanctuaries" for animals.

■ In a report for the Secretary of the Interior, a Special Advisory Board on Wildlife Management stated: "As originally conceived . . . all sport hunting [on the National Wildlife Refuge System] was prohibited."

■ 85 percent of monies to maintain the National Wildlife Refuge System come out of general tax revenues.

■ 95 percent to 96 percent of visitors to the refuge system do not hunt.

■ While 3.4 percent (3 million acres) of refuge was purchased with funds from the sale of duck stamps, a hunters' tax, that does not carry with it the right to hunt on National Wildlife Refuge System lands. Until 1949, there was no hunting at all on lands purchased with duck stamp funds. Removing NWRS lands from hunters would still leave them 1.5 *billion* acres available for public hunting (800 million acres of state- and federally-owned land; the remainder is privately owned but made available to hunters).

"Most of the hunters I saw or talked to had no respect or compassion for the birds or concern for what they were doing to them. There was no remorse over the cripples, the broken families of geese, or the wasted resource. Hunters repeatedly shot at geese over the line and at incoming flights when there was no possible chance for retrieving.

Time and time again I was shocked at the behavior of the hunters. I heard them laugh at the plight of the dazed cripples, which stumbled about. I saw them striking the heads of retrieved cripples against fenceposts."

—GLEN SHERWOOD, Interior Department biologist, from Audubon Magazine

One Simple Thing You Can Do to Help

32

✔ **You can help abolish hunting on National Wildlife Refuge lands** by supporting crucial legislation introduced by Representative Bill Green (R-NY), H.R. 1693, the Refuge Protection Act. If you write just three letters as a result of reading this book, you might consider making this one of them. While this may not be one of the greatest concentrations of animal abuse in terms of sheer number of animals killed and maimed, the current situation on our national refuges is an outrage we are ourselves tolerating—and financing. Our National Wildlife Refuge System ought to provide just that—refuge for beleaguered animal populations. It ought also to be a powerful symbol of all that is best in our relationship with the natural world; intead, it is a national scandal.

Below, you'll find a list of the forty-nine members of Congress who at the time of this writing have agreed to co-sponsor H.R. 1693. If your representative is listed here, please thank him or her for co-sponsoring the bill, and urge him or her to push for action on it. If your representative is not

"Species management, as practiced on wildlife refuges, does not allow animals to exist in a natural state because 'game' animals are managed to produce a surplus for hunting. This is at the expense of non-game species, including the predators who are a normal part of any wildlife ecosystem. This amounts to the destruction of biological diversity."

—LUKE A. DOMMER, president, Committee to Abolish Sport Hunting, from Animals' Agenda magazine listed, please ask him or her to help preserve the integrity of the National Wildlife Refuge System by closing it to hunting and trapping.

It is important to write to your senator as well: ask that a similar bill be introduced in the Senate.

CO-SPONSORS OF H.R. 1693, THE REFUGE PROTECTION ACT

Chester Atkins (D-MA)
Jim Bates (D-CA)
Anthony Beilenson (D-CA)
Charles Bennett (D-FL)
David Bonior (D-MI)
Robert Borski (D-PA)
Barbara Boxer (D-CA)
George Brown (D-CA)
Cardiss Collins (D-IL)
William Coyne (D-PA)
Ronald Dellums (D-CA)
Brian Donnelly (D-MA)
Bernard J. Dwyer (D-NJ)
Mervyn Dymally (D-CA)
Harris Fawell (R-IL)
Thomas Foglietta (D-PA)
Barney Frank (D-MA)
Charles Hayes (D-IL)
Andy Jacobs (D-IN)
Harry Johnston (D-FL)
Gerald Kleczka (D-WI)
Peter Kostmayer (D-PA)
Tom Lantos (D-CA)
William Lipinsky (D-IL)
Ron Machtley (R-RI)

Edward Markey (D-MA)
Robert Matsui (D-CA)
Nicholas Mavroules (D-MA)
Kweisi Mfume (D-MD)
Bruce Morrison (D-CT)
Robert Mrazek (D-NY)
Major Owens (D-NY)
Elizabeth Patterson (D-SC)
Nancy Pelosi (D-CA)
Charles Rangel (D-NY)
Arthur Ravenel, Jr. (R-SC)
Matthew Rinaldo (R-NJ)
Charles Rose (D-NC)
Jim Saxton (R-NJ)
James Scheuer (D-NY)
Claudine Schneider (R-RI)
Christopher Shays (R-CT)
Lawrence Smith (D-FL)
Pete Smith (R-VT)
Stephen Solarz (D-NY)
Edolphus Towns (D-NY)
Theodore S. Weiss (D-NY)
Alan Wheat (D-MO)
Sidney Yates (D-IL)

". . . the American public is footing the bill for predator-control programs that cause the systemic slaughter of thousands of additional refuge animals. Raccoons and red fox, squirrel and skunks are but a few of the many egg-eating predators trapped and destroyed in the name of 'wildlife management programs.' Seagulls are shot, fox pups poisoned, and coyotes killed by aerial gunners in low-flying aircraft. This wholesale destruction is taking place on the only Federal lands set aside to protect America's wildlife!"

—THE HUMANE SOCIETY OF THE UNITED STATES

MEAT MACHINES:
Intensive Confinement Factory Farming

"For most humans, especially for those in modern urban and suburban communities, the most direct form of contact with non-human animals is at meal time: we eat them. This simple fact is the key to what each one of us can do about changing these attitudes. The use and abuse of animals raised for food far exceeds, in sheer numbers of animals affected, any other kind of mistreatment."

—PETER SINGER

Old MacDonald's family farm has become an endangered species. Almost all the meat, milk, and eggs we buy today come from intensive confinement factory "farms." Conditions in these animal factories are the most shocking (and unhealthy) development in American agriculture ever.

Five *billion* animals suffer from birth to death on factory farms each year. More than 95 percent of all animal suffering in this country occurs in factory farming.

What Is Factory Farming?*

Imagine a world where traditional farms with fields and barnyards no longer exist. Where animals have become the immobilized machine parts of great automated assembly lines in darkened factories—tools whose sole purpose is to convert various feedstuffs, including some quite toxic substances, into flesh for human eating. Absolutely no consideration is given to the comfort of these animals, except to keep them alive in large enough numbers to make the animal factories profitable. Does all this sound like the ugly imaginings of a science fiction writer, a cynical vision of some future time?

It may surprise many people to know that this is exactly how more than five billion animals are raised for food in this country today; that the picture-book farm environments of yesterday are all but extinct; and that the lives of the creatures that we eat have become an endless horror dedicated to

---

Courtesy of the Coalition for Non-Violent Food, a project of Animal Rights International

filling the pockets of huge corporations. This affront to nature is called "Factory Farming" and it is an evil which we, as consumers, do have the power to change.

The Impact of Factory Farming on Your Health

"I know, in my soul, that to eat a creature who is raised to be eaten, and who never has a chance to be a real being, is unhealthy. It's like . . . you're just eating misery. You're eating a bitter life."

—ALICE WALKER

• *Forty to fifty percent of the antibiotics used in this country each year are administered, without medical supervision, to factory farmed animals. Other routine additions to animal feed include growth hormones, arsenic appetite stimulants, sulfa drugs, nitrofurans, coloring agents, fungicides, insecticides, and recycled waste.*

• *In a 1990 test of milk distributed in the New York City area, WCBS consumer affairs reporter Arnold Diaz reported that 80 percent of the milk tested contained tetracycline.*

• *A 1990 report by the United States Department of Agriculture revealed that 80 percent of the milk tested was contaminated by sulfa drugs.*

• *According to the USDA, at least one out of every fifty eggs in supermarkets is infected with live salmonella bacteria. (*Gourmet *magazine recently announced that because of the threat of salmonella poisoning, it will no longer print any recipe, such as mayonnaise, that calls for uncooked eggs.)*

• *Chicken parts, including intestines, are recycled into chicken feed. Industry experts allege that this may be a major factor in the now rampant epidemic of salmonella poisoning.*

• *The Enteric Diseases Branch of the National Centers for Disease Control estimates that between 400,000 and 4,000,000 cases of salmonella may occur each year* (2,500,000, we were told, is not an "unrealistic estimate"). A report on infectious disease published by the Carter Center—mentioned by the CDC as probably the most reliable information on salmonella mortality published so far—estimates that at least 500 people die unnecessarily each year from salmonella poisoning.*

• *One out of every three chickens sold in the supermarket is infected with live salmonella bacteria.*

---

*Science *magazine, 21 November 1986. "Drug Resistant Salmonella in the United States: An Epidemiological Study" by Cohen and Tauxe.*

• *The leading sources of pesticide residues in our diet are meat (55 percent) and dairy products (23 percent).*

• *Animals' Agenda recently reported that the FDA intercepted more chemically contaminated meat and milk in 1989 than in any year since 1986.*

• *Reducing consumption of meat, dairy products, and eggs by 50 percent can reduce the risk of heart attack by at least 45 percent.*

~~~~~~

"What happens {in slaughterhouses} to the fifteen million pounds of animal tissues which are too severely infected with cancer to be used? They are processed into hog and chicken feed. The result is a recycling of potential cancer substances repeatedly through the human and animal food chain."

—P. F. McGARGLE, World Magazine

Quoted in Animal Factories, *by Jim Mason and Peter Singer*

~~~~~~

Ecological Decimation*

■ 85 percent of the 4 million acres of topsoil lost in the United States each year is directly related to the raising of livestock.**

■ More than half the water consumed in the United States each year is used in factory farming.

■ 260 million acres of oxygen-producing trees have been cut down to create cropland to produce a meat-centered diet.

■ A 1978 Department of the Interior study, reported by Frances Moore Lappé, stated that "the value of raw materials consumed to produce food from livestock is greater than the value of all oil, gas, and coal consumed in this country."

■ Production of a single pound of meat requires 2,500 gallons of water. A pound of wheat can be produced with just 25 gallons.

■ 95 percent of the oats grown in this country are eaten by livestock. 80 percent of the corn grown here is eaten by livestock. 90 percent of its value as protein is wasted by cycling grain through livestock.

*Diet for a New America, by John Robbins; and Animal Factories, by Jim Mason and Peter Singer

**According to John Robbins, in Diet for a New America, topsoil is lost because we "force it artificially to supply the hyped-up demands we require to feed huge numbers of livestock."

■ Factory farm animals produce 250,000 pounds of excrement each second. Much of that winds up, untreated, in our streams and lakes—and in our groundwater.

■ The tropical rainforests of Central and South America, home to half of all the living species on earth, are being decimated to produce hamburger meat for fast-food restaurants. This loss of rainforest is responsible for most of the 1,000 species extinctions each year.

The Myth of "Milk-Fed" Veal

• *More than one million calves are raised each year for "gourmet" white-fleshed veal. The calves are the male offspring of Holstein cows used in milk production. More rarely, they are "excess" female Holstein calves.*

• *Calves are taken from their mothers soon after birth, some as early as one day, before they have a chance to ingest the colostrum they need to fend off disease. Calves with umbilical cords still attached are trucked to auctions, where, already stressed, they are exposed to opportunistic infection.*

• *Baby veal calves are tethered by the neck in veal crates measuring 24 to 28 inches by 54 to 60 inches; the crates are so narrow, calves cannot turn around or lie down and stretch. This is done because movement (the normal play of an inquisitive calf) would create muscle and decrease the "value" of the meat.*

• *For the duration of their lives the calves are given no water to drink. Nor are they given any solid food. Instead, to make sure that the flesh is "white" (anemic), they are fed milk "replacers" that are deliberately deficient in dietary iron, containing as little as one-tenth the iron needed to sustain minimal health. These replacers cause chronic diarrhea.*

• *Calves are not even provided with straw bedding, for fear that they will eat it (to get the small amount of iron in it) and turn their flesh pink. They are kept in darkness up to twenty-three hours a day.*

• *Housed in barns with up to 400 other crated calves, often with inadequate ventilation or sanitation systems, they are exposed to rampant infectious disease. As a matter of course, veal calves are given liberal, repeated doses of antibiotics. The Food Animal Concerns Trust (FACT) reported last year the case of a veterinarian in New Jersey who was charged with selling chloramphenicol (an antibiotic used in humans only when all else fails) to more than 500 veal producers. Chloramphenicol is banned from use in food animals because even a minute residue left in meat can cause a fatal blood disorder called aplastic anemia, in which bone marrow stops producing red blood cells; there is no way to predict which of us is susceptible to this disease.*

• No *antibiotics have been approved for use in veal calves. Because calves are denied any roughage, they metabolize drugs more slowly. According to FACT, "No data on residue* depletion rates are available for these calves. Producers must trust to luck in using medications. Their luck must have run out because for the first time in 1988 residues were monitored separately for fancy grade white veal: one in every thirty calves tested was found to have an illegal residue." The most common residues found were tetracycline, neomycin, and gentamicin.

• Veal calves are sent off to be slaughtered between the ages of fourteen to (at the most) twenty-two weeks. Most calves are slaughtered between the ages of sixteen and eighteen weeks.

• The irony is that all this stress, deprivation, and medication produces veal that has been evaluated as having no better flavor than conventional veal. It's just "white in color."

~~~~~~

"As a physician, I'm alarmed by the irresponsible use of antibiotics in so-called 'milk-fed' veal.

Today, nearly 50 percent of the antibiotics manufactured each year in the U.S. are poured directly into the feed of animals that are later eaten by humans. And for every ton of antibiotics fed to farm animals, we come that much closer to rendering these drugs worthless in fighting human illness.

The use of antibiotics in factory farming is creating a huge pool of mutant bacteria, resistant to antibiotics. These mutant bacteria infect human beings as well as animals.

The increase in drug-resistant bacteria is one of the most serious dilemmas facing medical doctors on a daily basis. In the hands of doctors, antibiotics can save human lives. But factory farms are abusing this precious medical resource—and all for a few cents' more profit on a pound of veal."

—KENNETH STOLLER, M.D., American Association for Science and Public Policy

~~~~~~

The Good News

■ Sweden's unprecedented animal welfare legislation, first enacted in July of 1988, effectively frees that country's animals from inhumane factory farming practices. Drugs and hormones are forbidden, except to treat disease. Biogenic manipulation is proscribed. Cattle now have the right to graze outdoors during the summer months. Pigs can no longer be tethered, have to be given bedding, and must be provided with separate areas for bedding and feeding. Chickens are to be taken out of battery cages. And fur farming will be so stringently regulated that observers are predicting the legislation could mean the end of Sweden's fur farm industry. Regulations will be phased in over a period of years.

- Effective January 1989, the European Economic Community has banned the importation of meat from any animals raised using synthetic hormones.
- In response to nationwide demonstrations, Burger King no longer serves veal sandwiches.
- Raley's Supermarkets, a 55-store chain in California, will no longer stock milk-fed veal.
- Reay's Ranch Markets stopped carrying milk-fed veal after protests by Concerned Arizonans for Animal Rights and Ethics.
- Restaurant owner Wolfgang Puck, proprietor of the trendy Spago, in Los Angeles, has stopped purchasing milk-fed veal out of concern for potential health risks to his patrons.
- The number of veal farms in Alberta, British Columbia, has decreased.
- Veal has been removed from the Ocean County, New Jersey, township high school cafeteria menu after a campaign begun by a student, Julie Viola. Julie worked from "the bottom up," first convincing students, who formed a student network against veal. They next approached homeroom teachers, the school principal, and the staff of the school cafeteria, educating each level as they went along.
- Bennigan's has removed veal from its restaurant menus nationwide.
- According to Nancy E. Wiswall, DVM, of the Humane Society of the United States, "1986 U.S. consumption of veal was only 1.6 pounds per person, down from 4.2 pounds per person in 1960."
- The Dutch government has banned the installation of new battery cages (row after row of tiny wire cages) for chickens, effective in 1994. The use of existing cages will become illegal in 2004.
- The Swiss ten-year phase-out period for battery caged hens will end on December 31, 1991. Most Swiss farmers have switched to the aviary system.

Frank Perdue's "Chicken Heaven"*

NOTE: *Frank Perdue is being singled out in advertisements paid for by animal rights groups and in the mass media because he has positioned himself as a leader of the chicken industry. Perdue has paid for and appears in advertising campaigns ("my chickens live in a house that's just chicken heaven"; they "eat better than you"; "your kids never had it so good") that conceal the realities of the cruel, unhealthy lives endured by factory-farmed chickens.*

*Courtesy Animal Rights International.

■ Life for the day-old Perdue chicken begins with painful dismember-ment as its beak is burned off with a hot knife (hot to cauterize the bleeding that ensues). Some chicks expire on the spot.

■ Perdue breeds today's "super-chicks" to grow ever faster on less feed. These juvenile giants grow so rapidly they have difficulty supporting their own weight and live out their lives on painfully crippled legs and feet.

■ Each chicken can expect to struggle through life with less than one square foot of living space. Typically, Perdue's contract growers crowd 25,000 birds into one long darkened shed. Mr. Perdue proudly markets his birds as "Oven Stuffers"™ but the bird in your oven may have four times the space it had when it was alive.

■ Unnatural overcrowding and filthy litter (not changed even once dur-ing the birds' lifetime) leads to suffocating and unhealthy conditions that often result in death and disease.

■ At about eight weeks of age the roughly five-pound birds are taken to one of Perdue's slaughter plants. Here, before their throats are slit, they are pinned upside down on a conveyer line and their heads are dragged through an electrified water trough. At least one veterinarian has observed that as many as a third survive the stunning process and approach the knife fully conscious; worse still, some enter the scalding tank alive.

■ Perdue is equally callous to his workers. National Public Radio (NPR), *The Washington Post,* and ABC's *20/20* report that Perdue workers were routinely fired after work-related injuries left them unable to function. And up to 30 percent of Perdue workers are afflicted with a crippling condition of the hands and wrists caused by having to butcher up to 75 chickens per minute.

■ Donna Bazemore, a former employee, told NPR she saw women uri-nating and vomiting on the work line because they were not allowed to leave it to go to the bathroom. And in 1986, Perdue admitted to the Pres-ident's Commission on Organized Crime that he sought help from orga-nized crime figures to keep it that way.

■ Perdue's has the dubious distinction of being the first company ever to be fined for water pollution by the Commonwealth of Virginia.

A Few More Chicken Facts

■ Almost 5 billion chickens are killed in this country each year for food.

■ More than half a million male chicks, of no value in the egg business, are thrown into large plastic garbage bags, where most suffocate within three hours. Some are ground up while still alive. The bodies are processed and used to feed animals captive in fur "farms."

■ Chicken feed is, of course, laced with antibiotics.

The Long Last Ride

NOTE: While it is not possible, because of space considerations, to describe the consistently abusive and unhealthy conditions endured by sheep, pigs, chickens used as "egg hens," cows, and other animals raised under factory farm conditions to satisfy our desire for meat, all the animals share one trauma in common: transportation to the slaughterhouse.

Transportation. There is virtually no protection under federal law for animals destined to be eaten. To quote the Humane Society of the United States' fact sheet, *Farm Animal Abuses During Transportation:* "While en route, cattle commonly develop a shipping fever, an often fatal respiratory malady. Many hogs are susceptible to Porcine Stress Syndrome, a severe reaction to stress that renders their meat pale, watery, and worthless. 'Downers' (animals which have fallen in the truck) and 'spreaders' (stock with back injuries or broken pelvises from rough handling) are unable to stand up and are trampled ... At termination points, a lack of equipment makes the humane removal of these creatures virtually impossible. Disabled animals are generally dragged by the legs, pulled with rope and chains, poked with electrical shocking devices, or simply beaten, kicked, or rolled off trucks."

Chickens. In the view of many industry experts, the worst of chickens' traumas are catchers and transportation. Catchers (who can barely breathe in the hideous chicken house air) grasp up to eight birds at a time and stuff the creatures into crates which are loaded onto trucks holding several thousand birds at a time. This catching process frequently results in dislocated hips and broken wings and legs. During the trip to the slaughter plant birds smother to death in the summer heat or freeze in the winter cold. Casualties, birds who die on the way to the slaughterhouse, are frequently sold to make pet food.

Stockyards. In 1982, 47 million cattle and calves passed through stockyards to be auctioned or privately sold on their way to fattening or "finishing" operations or to the slaughterhouse. According to the Humane Society of the United States: "Baby calves, just a few hours old, are picked up and thrown off unloading platforms, beaten with canes, jabbed with sticks, and kicked to goad them along. Adult animals, frightened and stressed by shouting and bright lights, and injured by slamming gates, are further abused by humans wielding 'hotshot' shocking devices, whips, and prods. Moving from one lighting extreme to another, animals become confused, frightened, and, again, the subjects of abusive handling. Hogs that have spent their entire lives in confinement with limited human contact are especially difficult to herd and handle, and thus become victims of rough and cruel treatment . . . 'Boar bashing,' or the breaking of a hog's nose with a heavy club or board, is done so the animal cannot smell other boars and initiate fights."

Six Simple Things You Can Do to Help **33–38**

✔ **Don't eat milk-fed veal.** Tell your friends and family not to eat milk-fed veal. Sometimes it helps if you give them a fact sheet or brochure on the subject to read. Most animal rights organizations have good veal pamphlets, including: Food Animal Concerns Trust, P.O. Box 14599, Chicago, IL 60614; The Humane Farming Association, 1550 California Street, Suite 12, San Francisco, CA 94109; Animal Rights Mobilization, P.O. Box 1553, Williamsport, PA 17703; People for the Ethical Treatment of Animals, P.O. Box 42516, Washington, DC 20015. You can use these same brochures to alert owners of local restaurants—and by all means take them to school, too, if yours is a school or college that still serves veal.

✔ **Eat less meat.** Better still, don't eat meat at all!

✔ **Seriously consider not eating meat at all.** The more informed you are about how animals are commercially raised and slaughtered in this country today, the harder it gets to sit down in good conscience and eat a slice of cow or lamb. Despite what you may have been taught in school, you do *not* need to eat meat to be healthy—or, for that matter, to have interesting, tasty meals. In fact, you can be a much healthier person if you do not eat meat, with considerably less chance of developing both heart disease and cancer. For example, a male American meat-eater has a 50 percent chance of having a heart attack; a male American pure vegetarian has a 4 percent chance of having a heart attack. There are currently an estimated twenty million people in this country who have, for reasons of health or ethics, given up eating animals. Two excellent books can help you to consider this decision: *Animal Factories* by Jim Mason and Peter Singer (Crown Publishers, 1980) and *Diet for a New America* by John Robbins (Stillpoint Publishing). The revised edition of Frances Moore Lappé's *Diet for a Small Planet* will also be of great help.

✔ **Don't eat factory-farmed eggs.** If you feel that you must keep on eating eggs, buy only free-range eggs. These are not impossible to find, even if you live in a big city. In New York City, for example, there are two vendors at the 14th Street Green Market who carry free-range eggs; one vendor has only sixteen chickens and, consequently, one has to arrive early in the morning to get the eggs. Another vendor has more chickens, but kills none of them and also raises legitimately grown organic vegetables.

✔ **If you feel that you must continue to eat chicken**—which, given, the unhealthy, filthy, disgusting manner in which factory farm chickens are raised, is difficult to understand—at least don't buy Perdue. Ask your friends, relatives, and co-workers not to buy Perdue. Talk to your local restaurant owners as well.

✔ **Participate in one of several meat-boycott days.** The Farm Animal Reform Movement sponsors an annual Great American Meatout, held each year on March 20, the first day of spring. In 1989, 55 groups in 33 states participated. In many areas of the country vegetarian feasts are part of the celebration, so this event can be a lot of fun. For more information, contact FARM (10101 Ashburton Lane, Bethesda, MD 20817). FARM also sponsors a World Farm Animals Day on October 2, Gandhi's birthday. The Humane Farming Association has also been sponsoring an annual National Veal Boycott Day, usually the third Friday in June. Contact them for more information: 1550 California Street, San Francisco, CA 94109, (415) 771-2253.

CLASSROOM DISSECTION:
You Don't Have to Do It

- *Every year, 5.7 million frogs, mice, rats, rabbits, chipmunks, sharks, pigs, cats, and dogs are dissected by junior and senior high school students.*
- *In Britain, under the British Education Act, students have the right to refuse to take part in dissections, and dissections are being phased out of the school system.*
- *In 1988, the state of California legislated that students in public schools who object to dissection on the grounds of conscience do not have to take part.*
- *The state of Maine now permits secondary students to opt out of dissection labs, as does the state of Pennsylvania.*

"The Woodstown-Pilesgrove (New Jersey) Board of Education has settled out of court with 15-year-old Maggie McCool, who sued over being flunked in science for refusing to dissect animals. The school must recalculate McCool's grades, pay her legal fees, and publish a statement in the student handbook exempting students from dissection if it infringes on their sincere religious beliefs."

—ANIMALS' AGENDA

Background

■ Dissection is included in the required curriculum of most high school biology and physiology classes, as well as college courses in biology, physiology, zoology, and comparative anatomy.

■ Animals bred or captured for dissection suffer the traumas of confinement, transport, callous handling, often inadequate food, and inhumane killing methods.

■ Cats and dogs are supplied by pounds and shelters, or are bred in puppy mills. Some have been procured by "bunchers" (see the chapter on pet theft, page 12)—and may be lost or stolen companion animals.

■ Chipmunks, frogs, sparrows, and snakes are collected from their natural environments. In the past, this has led to habitat destruction as well as severe imbalances: in Bangladesh, for example, so many frogs were captured for export for food and dissection that the unchecked insect population caused serious crop damage.

■ Frogs' spinal cords frequently are not properly severed ("pithed") before dissection. When this happens, frogs are dissected while still conscious.

■ Dissections teach students that animals' lives do not matter; it desensitizes students to the suffering of others.

■ Dissections have become a bizarre rite of passage, a kind of academic blood sport. For years, students whose sensibilities were offended by dissection were mocked by teachers and fellow students—in addition to being penalized if they did not participate in the ritual.

■ There are now numerous educational alternatives to dissection. These range from detailed computer simulations to models. (For sources of computer software, please see page 60.)

■ Dissections could effectively be phased out of virtually all junior and senior high school curricula within the next twenty-four months.

■ There's no reason why dissection could not be phased out of college curricula as well.

■ Many medical schools now permit students to choose alternatives to animal dissection.

39–46 Eight Simple Things You Can Do to Help

✔ **You should not allow yourself to be pressured into performing dissections in class.** However, before refusing to dissect, you must prepare yourself with effective arguments and also be prepared to suggest alternative projects. As part of that preparation, send for a copy of the booklet, *Objecting to Dissection: A Student Handbook,* published by the Animal Legal Defense Fund, 1363 Lincoln Avenue, San Rafael, CA 94901. Send $1 with your request. Their 9-step plan, "Saying No to Dissection," appears on page 57.

✔ **If you need advice about a situation in your junior or senior high school,** of if you have questions that need a faster reply, call the Dissection Hotline: (800) 922–FROG (3764).

✔ **If you are a college student (or teacher) on a campus where dissection is required,** you too can call the Dissection Hotline: (800) 922–FROG. You may also want a copy of the booklet, *Animals in Education: An Outline for Student Activists,* published by the American Anti-Vivisection Society, Suite 204—Noble Plaza, 801 Old York Road, Jenkintown, PA 19046–1685. Enclose $1 for the booklet.

✔ **To find an animal rights student group** near you, write to: Student Action Corps for Animals (SACA), P.O. Box 15588, Washington, DC 15588, (202) 543–8983.

✔ **If you are a college student thinking of applying to medical school,** choose a school that offers alternatives to dissection. A list of medical schools where students do not dissect or where alternatives to dissection are offered appears on page 61.

✔ **If you are a college student thinking of applying to veterinary school,** you can obtain a list of veterinary schools offering alternatives to dissection by writing to: Association of Veterinarians for Animal Rights (AVAR), 15 Dutch Street, Suite 500-A, New York, NY 10038–3779, (212) 962–7055.

✔ **If you are considering graduate school in psychology,** and have no interest in participation in torturous experiments on rats, cats, and primates, you can contact: Psychologists for the Ethical Treatment of Animals (PSYETA), P.O. Box 87, New Gloucester, ME 04260, (207) 926–4817. They'll recommend some graduate schools stressing non-animal investigative methods.

✔ **If you are a high school biology teacher using alternatives to dissection,** please share your methods with The National Association of Biology Teachers, c/o Rosaline Hairston, 11250 Roger Bacon Drive, #19, Reston, VA 22090.

And with Just a Little More Effort You Could . . .

✔ **If you are a parent with children heading toward or currently in high school,** now would be a good time to strongly suggest to your local school administration, as well as your PTA, the need to eliminate dissection.

Saying No to Dissection: A 9-Step Plan*

I. Know Yourself. Examine your motives and decide how far you are prepared to go in order to establish your right not to dissect. Are you willing to present your case to your teacher and principal? Find your own alternatives? Take legal action? Accept your own limitations given the risks involved and adjust your goals accordingly?

2. Ask Questions Early. Before the term starts, or as soon as possible thereafter, ask your teacher whether you will be required to dissect or use live animals. Find out precisely what you will be required to do. Don't rely on your teacher to give you advance warning.

3. Voice Objections Early. Tell your teacher of your intention not to participate in dissection experiments as soon as possible; do not wait until the day of the dissection assignment to voice your objection. This will give both you and your teacher enough time to work out an acceptable alternative.

4. Be Firm, Be Calm. State your objections calmly and clearly, and be prepared to discuss your reasons for refusing to dissect. Never approach your teacher in an arrogant, self-righteous, or confrontational manner. Presume that he or she has a different belief system on the issue of animal use, and it is unlikely that you will change those views. On the other hand, stress

*Courtesy of The Animal Legal Defense Fund

that you do not wish this value system to be imposed upon you, as it conflicts with your ethical or spiritual beliefs.

5. Suggest Alternatives. Suggest reasonable alternatives that will meet the teaching goals of the course by some method that doesn't involve the harmful use of animals. This could include writing a paper, preparing anatomical charts, or studying diagrams, videos, or models. The alternative project should take an equivalent amount of time and effort. Be prepared to be tested on the same material as other students, as long as the test itself does not include a practical dissection, or the use of dissected specimens.

You should not be penalized for doing an alternative project. If you need specific suggestions for alternative course work, check the "Alternatives to Animal Dissection" section that follows, or call the Dissection Hotline [(800) 922-FROG].

6. Ask for a Straight Answer. Ask your teacher to respond promptly to your request for an alternative project so you'll have enough time to complete it. If you get a noncommittal or negative response, don't hesitate to take your request to the principal or another appropriate administrator.

7. Get a Parent's Support. If your teacher is unresponsive to your objections and suggested alternatives, ask your parents to get involved. While this is certainly not necessary, the presence of a supportive parent can sometimes make teachers or administrators more accommodating. The backing of your local PTA can also be very helpful.

8. Organize Others. Another approach is to organize like-minded students and approach your teacher as a group. Use the school media, newspaper, etc., as a forum for discussion. Introduce the ethical issues surrounding dissection at student government meetings and in classroom discussions.

9. Get Legal Advice. The Animal Legal Defense Fund has had great success in negotiating with educational institutions on this issue. If you want legal advice or need to take legal action to defend your right to object to dissection, the Dissection Hotline can put you in touch with an ALDF attorney.

"Students who refuse dissection are breaking new ground in changing human attitudes about whether animal lives can merely be used and thrown away. . . . Students who refuse dissection are refusing the act of animal exploitation and refusing the learned mindset that allows school-sponsored animal exploitation to be considered normal and necessary."

—ROSA FELDMAN, Student Action Corps for Animals, quoted in Animals' Agenda

---

Alternatives to Animal Dissection*

There are many alternatives to animal dissection as a method of teaching biology, anatomy, or zoology. Here are some teaching materials you can suggest to your teacher, principal, or administrator. If you have a specific question or need that is not answered by this list, contact the toll-free Dissection Hotline at (800) 922-FROG (3764).

Some of the videotapes and books show images of dissected animals. While we do not advocate the dissection of any animal, some students and teachers might find these materials appropriate and preferable to dissecting live animals in the classroom.

VIDEOTAPES AND SLIDES

These videotapes cover the internal and external structures of the frog and compare them to human structures.

The Frog Inside-Out. Instructivision, Inc., 3 Regent Street, Livingston, NJ 07039, (201) 992-9081.

Frog Dissection Explained. Bergwall Productions, 106 Charles Lindbergh Productions, Uniondale, NY 11553, (800) 645-3565.

Dissection of the Frog. JLM Visuals, 920 7th Avenue, Grafton, WI 53024, (414) 377-7775.

ANATOMICAL MODELS, CHARTS, AND OTHER LEARNING TOOLS

Plastic models, charts, and a variety of resources are available from the following biological supply houses. You can either call or write for their catalogs.

Carolina Biological Supply Company (CBSC), 2700 York Road, Burlington, NC 27215, (800) 334-5551. Resources include reusable zoology slide sets, diagrams, transparencies, filmstrips, and models of many frequently dissected animals, as well as diagrams, charts, and models of human anatomy.

Denoyer-Geppert Science Company, 5215 North Ravenswood Avenue, Chicago, IL 60640, (800) 621-1014. Numerous charts and models of human and non-human animals. Biology test sheets of many animals with line drawings and anatomical parts for identification by the student are also available.

*Courtesy of The Animal Legal Defense Fund

Nystrom, Division of Herff Jones, Inc., 3333 Elston Avenue, Chicago, IL 60618, (800) 621-8086. Resources include laminated study prints of anatomy that students mark for hands-on involvement; plastic zoological models of dissected perch, frogs, earthworms, and grasshoppers; zoology charts of many commonly dissected animals and human anatomy and physiology charts.

Ward's Natural Science Establishment, Inc. (WNSE), 5100 West Henrietta Road, P.O. Box 92912, Rochester, NY 14692, (800) 962-2660. Many dissection alternatives, including prepared microscope slides of numerous animal cells and tissues, anatomy models, filmstrips of dissection, slide sets of photos of whole and dissected animals, slides of live animals in their natural environments, laminated "Dissectogram" cards with color photographs of dissections, and biology charts of numerous human and non-human animals.

COMPUTER PROGRAMS

Operation Frog. Available for Apple II and Commodore 64 computers from Scholastic Software, Inc., P.O. Box 7502, 2931 E. McCarty Street, Jefferson City, MO 65102, (800) 541-5513. Simulated lab dissection and reconstruction of a frog. Organs are removed, using proper sequence and instruments, and viewed in detail. Upcoming versions will include dog, cat, rabbit, gerbil, and other animals.

Visifrog by Ventura. Available from CBSC. For the Apple II. Presents anatomical structures of the frog in high resolution color graphics, with practice in identifying names of structures and functions.

Cambridge Development Laboratory's Educational Software. Available from Cambridge Development Laboratory, 214 Third Avenue, Waltham, MA 02154, (800) 637-0047. Catalog features a large selection of computer programs (for Apple II, Commodore 64, and IBM PC) that can replace the harmful use of animals for elementary through college students. Areas covered include General Biology and Botany, Biochemistry, Genetics, Population Dynamics, Physiology, and Anatomy.

Software for dissection labs. Available from WNSE. For use with Apple II and IIe of earthworms, clams, crayfish, grasshoppers, starfish, perch, and frogs.

Biology dissection guides. Available from CBSC. For computers. Describe and display dissection procedures step-by-step, with review questions. For starfish, earthworms, clams, crayfish, grasshoppers, perch, or frogs. Use with Apple II.

MEDICAL SCHOOLS WITH NO ANIMAL LABS*

Hahnemann University, Philadelphia, PA
Howard University, Washington, DC
Louisiana State University, Shreveport, LA
Mercer University, Macon, GA
Michigan State University, East Lansing, MI (5 of 6 campuses)
New York University, New York, NY
Ohio State University, Columbus, OH
SUNY Stony Brook, Stony Brook, NY
Tufts University, Boston, MA
University of Maryland, Baltimore, MD
University of Michigan, Ann Arbor, MI
University of Washington, Seattle, WA

MEDICAL SCHOOLS WITH OPTIONAL ANIMAL LABS
(NOT A REGULAR PART OF THE CURRICULUM)*

Albert Einstein College of Medicine, Bronx, NY
Brown University, Providence, RI
Case Western Reserve University, Cleveland, OH
Columbia University, New York, NY
Creighton University, Omaha, NE
Duke University, Durham, NC
George Washington University, Washington, DC
Medical College of Georgia, Augusta, GA
Medical College of Pennsylvania, Philadelphia, PA
Michigan State University, East Lansing, MI (1 of 6 campuses)
Nebraska University, Omaha, NE
Penn State College of Medicine, Hershey, PA
St. Louis University, St. Louis, MO
Stanford University, Palo Alto, CA
Vanderbilt University, Nashville, TN
Wright State University, Dayton, OH
University of Hawaii, Honolulu, HI
University of Illinois, Chicago, IL
University of Minnesota, Duluth, MN
University of Wisconsin, Madison, WI

NOTE: Due to changing policies at educational institutions, this list is expected to change frequently. If you know of any changes, additions, or deletions that will need to be made, please contact: Physicians Committee for Responsible Medicine, P.O. Box 63221, Washington, DC 20015, (202) 686-2210.

Courtesy of the Physicians Committee for Responsible Medicine

BOOKS

Modern Biology, Holt, Rinehart and Winston, Inc., 1989, Teacher's Edition. This new textbook does not include dissections, in order to "foster a greater respect for living organisms."

General Zoology Lab Guide—Complete Version, by J. E. Wodsedalke and Charles F. Lytle. Available from WNSE. Photographs include those taken with electron microscopes to reflect the latest knowledge of animal structure and function.

Grzimek's Animal Life Encyclopedia. Available from CBSC or WNSE. A set of thirteen volumes of animal types (i.e., insects, fishes/amphibians and mammals) with photos, detailed illustrations, and plates with acetate overlays of anatomy.

The Frog Book, by Mary C. Dickerson. Available from WNSE. Full coverage of frog physiology.

The Anatomy Coloring Book, by W. Kapit and L. M. Elson. Available from HarperCollins Publishers, P. O. Box 1610, Hagerstown, MD 21741 (800) 638-3030. Contains detailed illustrations of human systems and anatomy, with 142 plates of line illustrations.

Zoology Coloring Book, L. M. Elson. Available from HarperCollins Publishers, P. O. Box 1610, Hagerstown, MD 21741, (800) 638-3030. Detailed plates of invertebrate and vertebrate animal anatomy.

Laboratory anatomy and dissection books of rats, rabbits, cats, and fetal pigs. Available from CBSC and WNSE.

NON-ANIMAL PROJECTS

Alternative Project Sheets is a collection of specific alternatives to some of the most common animal-related biology experiments and dissections. Available from the National Association for Humane and Environmental Education (NAAHEE), Box 362, East Haddam, CT 06423.

The Harvard Biometer can replace frog pithing to study heart functions. It provides students with exercises associated with the study of the cardiovascular system, harmlessly using the students instead of frogs. The electric Biometer amplifies the heart sounds and wrist pulses of the students to demonstrate cardiac bioelectric signals. Available from Phipps & Bird, Inc., 8741 Landmark Road, Box 27324, Richmond, VA 23261, or call (800) 446-1509 and ask for the pamphlet called *Studying Bioelectricity and Cardiography,* by T. Daniel Kimbrough, Ph.D.

The Endangered Species Handbook, by Greta Nilsson. Contains numerous non-animal lab projects. Available from The Animal Welfare Institute, P.O. Box 3650, Washington, DC 20007, for $5.

HUMANE EDUCATION:
Teaching Compassion

Background*

■ Despite existing mandates, humane education is not a requirement for pre-service training and teacher certification.

■ College professors admit to being unfamiliar with the underlying philosophy, methodology, and resources.

■ Humane education is not infused into teacher training. In-service training is not provided for classroom teachers.

■ Resource materials are not provided to implement the mandate.

■ Formal on-site verification of compliance is nonexistent.

■ Significant humane education questions are not included on standardized tests.

■ Dissections are required as part of the educational curricula for high schools in forty-seven states.

■ High school science fairs continue to reward students for redundant, cruel, or senseless "experiments" involving live animals.

■ But in twenty-three states, instruction in the humane treatment and protection of animals at the primary and secondary school levels has been mandated by educational laws.

"To date, funding initiatives, policy directives, and verification of compliance are minimal to non-existent. Instead, students are routinely conditioned to become accepting of the status quo. For the most part animal-welfare/rights perspectives are effectively censored from mainstream educational presentations."

—SHEILA SCHWARTZ, Chairperson, New York City Central Board of Education Humane Education Committee

---

*From "Institutionalizing Humane Innovations in Educational Institutions," by Sheila Schwartz, Humane Innovations and Alternatives in Animal Education

✔ **Individual classroom teachers** can incorporate animal rights issues and materials into their lesson plans. English teachers might add one or two books on animal rights issues (William Kotzwinkle's novel, *Dr. Rat,* for example). Social Studies teachers might wish to do a unit on events leading to and following the Aspen referendum to ban fur, or look at the animal rights movement as a grass roots movement for political and social change.

✔ **Individual students** should read the previous chapter, "Dissection: You Don't Have to Do It."

And with Just a Little More Effort You Could . . .

✔ **Boycott.** Teachers, students, and parents should boycott participation in science fairs sponsored by the International Science and Engineering Fair (ISEF), administered by Science Service, 1719 N Street, NW, Washington, DC 20036. ISEF retains rules that permit untrained students to perform surgery on animals, as well as administer toxic substances. So far, ISEF has resisted pressure to make its rules more humane.

✔ **Parents should urge teachers,** school administrators, and PTAs to make humane education a more integral part of everyday education.

✔ **Humane groups/teachers' groups must lobby** and convince central boards of education and local teachers' unions that humane education must be a priority. This can be achieved via letters, petitions, telegrams, and postcards.

Useful Humane Education Materials for Teachers

■ For alternatives to dissection see the previous chapter, "Dissection: You Don't Have to Do It."

■ Audiovisual materials for classroom use can be borrowed from the Marin County (California) Humane Society, (415) 883-3522.

■ Complete teaching units on wildlife, pets, and farm animals are available for levels K–2 and 3–5, $6 each, from the Ohio Humane Education Association, P.O. Box 546, Grove City, OH 43146.

■ After extensive lobbying efforts, the New York City Board of Education has created an excellent *Humane Education Resource Guide* (1985), for use in primary schools. This is available free on request to NYC public school educators, $6 to other educators. Contact: Humane Education Committee, P.O. Box 445, New York, NY 10028, (212) 410-3095.

■ People and Animals: A Humane Education Curriculum Guide is available from the National Association for the Advancement of Humane and Environmental Education, 67 Salem Road, East Haddam, CT 06423. Level B is for first and second grades; Level C, third and fourth; Level D, fifth and sixth. $7 each. See its publications catalog for other humane teaching materials.

■ The Trapping of Wildlife, or, What Really Happens in the Woods? is a terrific assembly program (Series 101) published by Friends of Animals, P.O. Box 1244, Norwalk, CT 06856. Included are follow-up questions and answers to those questions.

■ Educators wishing to form humane education committees can call or write: Ms. M. Carole Bollini, 9 Powell Road, Allendale, NJ 07401, (201) 934-0470. Carole is a member of the New York City Central Board of Education Humane Education Committee and will provide useful advice.

■ High school biology teachers may want to send for a copy of *Alternatives to Current Uses of Animals in Research, Safety Testing, and Education: A Layman's Guide,* available from The Humane Society of the United States, 2100 L Street, NW, Washington, DC 20037.

THE TRIUMPH
OF A CONSUMER BOYCOTT:
Putting an End to Purse Seine Netting of Dolphins

The week that we were completing work on this book, Anthony J. F. O'Reilly, chairman of the H.J. Heinz Company, owner of the Star-Kist brand of tuna, announced that his company would no longer buy tuna caught in purse seine nets that also trap and kill dolphins. While being interviewed by reporters, Mr. O'Reilly said that the company was greatly influenced in its decision by pressure from consumers and from restaurant chains like Blimpie's.

Star-Kist currently holds a market share of more than one-third of the canned tuna sold in the United States. Mr. O'Reilly admitted that he hopes this decision, combined with a new "dolphin safe" label, will increase Star-Kist's sales. Heinz was later that day joined in its decision by the Van Camp Seafood Company, which markets Chicken of the Sea tuna, and Bumble Bee Seafoods, Inc. Together, the three companies sell 70 percent of the canned tuna in the United States.

The sponsors of the tuna boycott, Earth Island Institute and Greenpeace, deserve our sincere appreciation for their efforts. Biologist Sam LaBudde's undercover work on a tuna fishing boat provided the solid documentation—and documentary footage—that influenced so many people's decisions.

Yet, while there are good reasons for celebration—fishing for tuna "on dolphin" has cost the lives of 6.5 million dolphins over the past 30 years—there is still work to be done. Representative Barbara Boxer has proposed legislation that would force *all* tuna canners to label their product as "dolphin safe"—or not. And there are still plenty of foreign fishing vessels which will continue using the unconscionable purse seine method of fishing for tuna.

Background

■ During 1987 alone, as many as 115,000 dolphins were drowned by purse seine netting for tuna in the eastern tropical Pacific.

■ Dolphins are gentle, intelligent, warm-blooded mammals with highly developed brains slightly larger than our own.

■ Dolphins have always maintained a benign, playful relationship with humans.

■ For reasons as yet undetermined, yellowfin tuna school below groups of dolphins, which must swim to the surface to breathe.

■ Commercial tuna fishermen use sightings of breaking groups of dolphins as a cue to begin their kill.

■ Frightened dolphins are chased and herded together using speedboats and helicopters; underwater grenades are used to disorient the dolphins and make them draw closer together.

■ Huge nets are used to pull up both tuna and dolphin. The dolphins, including nursing and pregnant females, panic and drown, or are entangled and crushed to death by net retrieval machinery.

■ 100 times more dolphins than whales have been killed each year, yet the United States government has persisted in allowing U.S. and foreign fleets to continue killing dolphins.

■ The killing of dolphins is not accidental. It is deliberate.

✔ **Don't eat tuna.** Tuna are sentient creatures, too, and feel fear and pain.

✔ **If you make the decision to continue to eat tuna,** at least buy only canned tuna labeled "Dolphin Safe." If you're eating in a restaurant, ask if they use dolphin-safe tuna.

✔ **Call Heinz and tell them you think they made the right decision.** The number is 412-237-5757. Ask for Edward Smyth, director of corporate affairs. You might also want to write to Mr. O'Reilly:

Mr. Anthony O'Reilly
CEO
H. J. Heinz Co.
USX Building, 60th Floor
600 Grant
Pittsburgh, PA 15219

And with Just a Little More Effort You Could . . .

✔ **High school and college students.** Ask that your school cafeteria use only dolphin-safe tuna.

✔ **Support the Dolphin Protection Consumer Information Act,** H.R. 2926, first introduced by Representative Barbara Boxer during the 101st Congress. The bill would require that tuna products (including generic brands) be labeled in a way that would enable consumers to differentiate between "dolphin-safe" and "dolphin-deadly" products. Hearings were held by the House Merchant Marine and Fisheries Committee's Subcommittee on Fisheries and Wildlife Conservation and the Environment; despite 128 co-sponsors, no action was taken. Now is the time to write to your congressperson about the proposed Act. Reminder: If you don't know who your legislators are, call your local League of Women Voters.

✔ **Write to Commerce Secretary Robert Mosbacher** to ask for strict enforcement of the Marine Mammal Protection Act. So far, Mosbacher has been notoriously unsympathetic to animal rights/conservation issues, but perhaps he'll listen to public opinion this time:

Mr. Robert Mosbacher
Secretary of Commerce
Commerce Building
14th Street, NW
Washington, DC 20230

DRIFTNETS: Stripmining the Seas

- *In the last 10 years, plastic driftnets forty miles long have taken a greater toll on the North Pacific than all other fishing and whaling combined.*
- *For six months of every year, May through October, more than one thousand fishing vessels deploy 30,000 to 40,000 miles of net each working day in the North Pacific—enough net to circle the planet.*
- *After each night's work, up to 85 percent of the catch is thrown away as non-marketable "trash."*
- *Monster nets deployed in the Pacific by fleets from Japan, Taiwan, and South Korea have decimated populations of dolphins, sea turtles, marlin, tuna, swordfish, American salmon, seals, sunfish, and baby humpback whales.*
- *Anywhere from 500,000 to 750,000 sea birds die in driftnets each year.*
- *At the end of each season, a single driftnetting vessel can bring back to port enough frozen fish to gross $500,000 to $2,000,000.*

Background

■ The Asian fishing fleet is in pursuit of red squid, albacore and skip-jack tuna, North American salmon, and marlin.

■ The driftnets they use are made of 2-inch diameter, fine, monofilament nylon mesh that is almost impossible to see underwater, especially at night. Each driftnet can extend 30–45 feet deep and 50 miles in length.

■ The Asian driftnet fleet has been banned from operation within the coastal waters of virtually every nation in the Pacific basin, including Japan.

■ More than 150 driftnetting vessels are currently stripping the waters off Australia and New Zealand. According to Merritt Clifton, writing in

Animals' Agenda, "the driftnetters are believed to be taking from 35,000 to 60,000 tons of albacore tuna from the region, while the sustainable yield . . . is only 15,000 tons."

■ Driftnets are also being used with devastating effects in the Mediterranean.

■ In 1987, the Driftnet Impact Monitoring Act was passed by Congress, but was never allocated any funding. Driftnet fleets continue to operate unregulated and unobserved.

■ In 1988, the United States Supreme Court upheld an earlier decision, banning Japanese driftnets from the North Pacific.

One Simple Thing You Can Do to Help   52

✔ **This is one of those cases where only letter writing will do.** This time let's start with the president (please see the sample letter below).

President George S. Bush
The White House
Washington, DC 20500

Dear Mr. President:

During the last ten years, driftnet fishing has taken a greater toll on the North Pacific than all other fishing and whaling combined. Huge nets deployed in the Pacific by fleets from Japan, Taiwan, and South Korea have decimated populations of dolphins, sea turtles, marlin, tuna, swordfish, American salmon, seals, sunfish, and baby humpback whales. Between 500,000 and 750,000 sea birds die in driftnets each year.

As you know, the Asian driftnet fleet has been banned from operation within the coastal waters of virtually every nation in the Pacific basin, including Japan. Yet the Asian driftnet fleet, which is at least fifty percent Japanese-owned, continues to stripmine the seas of the North Pacific.

I urge you to request that the Secretary of State do everything in his power to seek an international agreement to ban the use of driftnet fishing on the high sea.

Very respectfully yours,

Anna Sequoia

Also write to your congressperson to request that he or she support H.R. 2958, the Marine Resource Protection & Driftnet Use Cessation Act, introduced by Congressman Unsoeld of Washington. You can use exactly the same letter as the one we've drafted for President Bush, except substitute this last paragraph:

> *I urge you to support H.R. 2958, the Marine Resources Protection & Driftnet Use Cessation Act. This act requires that the Secretary of State seek to secure an international agreement to ban the use of driftnet fishing on the high sea.*

~~~~~~

"The increasing and widespread use of driftnetting may soon cause the regional extinction of some species leading ultimately to the biological collapse of large areas of the planet's marine ecosystems."

—SAM LABUDDE, Earth Island Journal

~~~~~~

THE LAST WHALES:
Breaching in a Lonely Sea

~~~~~~

"I have spent the last eleven years studying right whales in Argentina and I have felt each year a great loneliness of spirit when the whales leave and the bay returns to silence and emptiness. It is hard to convey that feeling but when the whales are there and our days are spent watching them breaching, spouting, swimming, courting, sailing, pushing, and shoving—all at their majestic, glacial pace; or when I see them suspended and floating in the shallows, great cloudlike beings drifting with currents too slow to perceive, my spirits soar and I am moved in ways that nothing which is smaller ever moves me."

—DR. ROGER PAYNE, *from his acceptance speech of the Animal Welfare Institute's 1980 Albert Schweitzer Medal for himself and his wife, Katharine*

~~~~~~

The Statistics

• *In a recently completed, decade-long survey off the coast of Antarctica, only 453 blue whales were found in an area where scientists expected to find ten times as many.*

- Despite 20 years of protection, the world population of blue whales has dropped from 200,000 to between 600 and (at most) 2,200.
- Only 4,000 fin whales survive below the equator.
- The Draft National Recovery Plan for the Right Whale estimates that because of past hunting, there are no more than 600 Right Whales left.
- In 1986, Japan refused to recognize the International Whaling Commission's moratorium on whaling and killed over 10,000 whales.
- In 1989, Japan killed 39,000 Dall's porpoises (of a population of 105,000). They said they were compelled to do so because of consumer demand for whale meat, and because of restrictions on the number of whales they could kill.
- In 1990, Japan plans to kill 400 minke whales (the smallest of the great whales), under the guise of "scientific research."
- Norway plans to kill 20 minke whales in 1990, using the same lame excuse.
- The Danish dependency of the Faroe Islands will slaughter (for sport, using harpoons and grappling hooks) up to 2,300 pilot whales during the species' annual migration past that region. Thirty to fifty percent of the meat will be discarded in city dumps.

"There's an emotional issue that has the potential to harm Japan greatly—the issue of the environment. There is growing news coverage of Japan's role in the loss of endangered species, in the practices of drift-net fishing and tropical logging. No country is without blame when it comes to the environment, but Japan will come under increasing pressure, perhaps even the boycott of Japanese products."
—FORMER PRESIDENT RONALD REAGAN, *in a 1989 speech to Japanese business leaders*

Background

■ More whales were killed during this century than during all previous centuries combined.

■ As far back as the 1930s, it was recognized that overhunting was having disastrous consequences. In 1930–1931 alone, almost 30,000 blue whales were taken. The bowhead and gray whales were virtually wiped out. As a consequence, several international agreements were reached, including one sponsored by the League of Nations. Japan abided by none of these.

■ In 1971, the U.S. Department of the Interior placed eight species of great whales on its list of endangered foreign wildlife. This effectively cut off the U.S. market, consumers of 20 percent of the world's whale products.

■ Despite reductions over the past 20 years in sheer numbers of whales killed, establishment of a few sanctuaries in the Indian Ocean and protection of several calving grounds, many remaining whale populations teeter on the brink of extinction.

■ In 1982, the International Whaling Commission (IWC) adopted a moratorium on commercial whaling. Whaling nations were allowed three years to comply with this moratorium.

■ In a poll conducted that year by Nippon Research Center, Ltd., the Japanese section of the Gallup organization, 76 percent of Japanese interviewed said they believe their country should abide by the decision of the IWC.

■ In 1984, Japan signed an agreement with the United States, in which it promised to end all whaling by 1988. In return, the U.S. agreed not to impose the economic sanctions authorized under U.S. law.

■ Japan, Norway, and Iceland continued to conduct commercial whaling until 1989. Toward the end of that period they simply called their commercial catch "scientific research."

THE CULTURAL MYTH ABOUT WHALE MEAT IN JAPAN*

The whaling industry greatly exaggerates the importance of whale meat today by attempting to link oldstyle whaling that occurred in a few coastal villages to the modern industrial whale slaughter. Middle-aged people in Japan represent the only generation in the nation's history that has widely consumed whale meat. During the difficult period immediately following World War II, many schoolchildren were fed whale meat because it was a cheap source of protein.

Several major whaling companies competed for this market by building increasingly efficient whaling ships. Their combined production of whale meat, however, vastly exceeded public demand. In order to protect their investments, these companies developed ways to use large amounts of whale meat in bland-tasting "fish sausages" and other products. During the peak of the whaling in the 1950s and 1960s, Japan actually exported several million pounds of lower quality whale meat to the U.S. for use as a pet food.

*Courtesy of Greenpeace

✔ **Stay informed.** At the time we go to press, it is impossible to predict the outcome of the 1990 meeting of the International Whaling Commission, which is scheduled to review the worldwide ban on commercial whaling. To stay informed, see the latest issues of *Animals' Agenda* or *The Animals' Voice* magazines. Or write to: Cetacean Society International, P.O. Box 9145, Wethersfield, CT 06109; or Greenpeace, 1436 U Street, NW, Suite 201-A, Washington, DC 20009; or Sea Shepherd Conservation Society, Box 7000, Redondo Beach, CA 90277; or Save Our Whales Campaign, Animal Welfare Institute, P.O. Box 3650, Washington, DC 20007.

✔ **Boycott Norwegian fish products.** This boycott has been called by the Sea Shepherd Conservation Society, Box 48446, Vancouver, BC V7X 1A2. Specifically, it protests the brutal slaughter for sport of thousands of pilot whales by the Faroe Islanders. As described in a 1985 report by Jennifer Gibson and Dave Currey (the first documented account of this annual ritual): "As the whales approach the shore, the animal at the rear of the pod is stabbed behind the dorsal fin with a spear, causing it to swim in its agony through the pod towards the beach. The other whales will follow, beaching themselves in the shallow water. The hooks are then sunk into the whales' heads and used to drag them up on the beach by those working from the shore. A cut is made into the whale's spinal marrow through the blubber and flesh, a hands-breath behind the blowhole with the knife. This causes the whale to thrash violently and break its own spinal cord." To protest, write:

Prime Minister Atli P. Dam
Hjemmestyret, Thorshayn
Faeroe Islands

✔ **Boycott Japan Air Lines.** This boycott is being sponsored by Boycott for the Whales, a coalition of environmental and animal welfare organizations, 2007 R Street, NW, Washington, DC 20009. JAL has been chosen because JAL's major shareholder, with almost 40 percent of the stock, is the Japanese government. Not many of us will have the opportunity to participate in this boycott (how often do we fly to Japan or the Orient?)— but your corporation may book people on JAL, and your travel agent may be doing the same: talk to them. If you do have the opportunity to help the boycott, let JAL know:

Mr. Yasumoto Takagi
President
Japan Air Lines, Tokyo Bldg.
7-3, Marunouchi 2-chome
Chiyoda-ku, Tokyo 100
Japan.

✔ **Telephone your local Japanese consulate** and tell them (try to be polite) how you feel about their continued whaling.

Washington, DC (202) 234-2266	New Orleans, LA (504) 529-2101
Houston, TX (713) 652-2977	Atlanta, GA (404) 892-2700
Portland, OR (503) 221-1811	Seattle, WA (206) 682-9107
San Francisco, CA	Honolulu, HI (808) 536-2226
(415) 777-3533	Chicago, IL (312) 280-0400
Los Angeles, CA (213) 624-8305	Boston, MA (617) 973-9772
Anchorage, AK (907) 279-8428	New York, NY (212) 371-8222

And with Just a Little More Effort You Could . . .

✔ **Write to President Bush,** and ask him to embargo Japanese fish in response to Japanese whaling. You can reach him at: The White House, Washington, DC 20500.

✔ **Help establish the Stellwagon Bank as a National Marine Sanctuary.** If you work or go to school someplace where you can get petitions signed, write to: Cetacean Society International, P.O. Box 9145, Wethersfield, CT 06109, and ask for a Stellwagon Petition, plus information about their Stellwagon Sanctuary drive.

Even More Proof That Boycotts Work

Greenpeace, co-sponsor of the international boycott of Icelandic fish (until 1989, Iceland continued "scientific research" whaling), has—at least for the moment—called off the boycott. According to Greenpeace, the boycott—during which individual restaurant chains like Long John Silver's, Red Lobster, and Shoney's, plus some school systems as well as the City of Boston, refrained from purchasing Icelandic fish—"cost the Icelandic fishing industry some $50,000,000."

At the 1989 session of the International Whaling Commission, Iceland said that it would call off its whaling during 1990. Whether Iceland continues this policy of restraint in the years to come remains to be seen.

SEA TURTLES: The Shrimp Connection

- *Throughout the past decade, more than 11,000 endangered sea turtles drowned in funnel-like shrimp fishing nets each year.*
- *Turtle Extruder Devices (TEDs)—a simple, cagelike device that deflects turtles out the top with diagonal bars—could save virtually all turtles now being killed during shrimping operations.*
- *Turtle Extruder Devices are inexpensive ($25–$400).*

"*I don't care if the law's in effect or not. I just ain't gonna use a goddamn TED. I been shrimpin' since 1972, and I don't want a bunch of Washington politicians tellin' me how to catch shrimp.*"

—*JIMMY ("Like hell I'm gonna tell you my last name"), Louisiana shrimper*
Quoted in Striking Back, *official newsletter of the Reptile Defense Fund*

Background

■ For more than 100 million years, sea turtles have returned from the open seas to bear their young on the same beaches where they were born.

■ After 10 years of study and delay, during which TEDs received 24,000 hours of testing by the Commerce Department, in 1989 U.S. District Court Judge Thomas Hogan ordered shrimpers to use Turtle Excluder Devices.

■ Just weeks after the order by Judge Hogan, Commerce Secretary Robert Mosbacher suspended TED regulations. "Commerce Secretary Mosbacher's highly irresponsible suspension of TED regulations for nearly an entire shrimping season," stated Peter A. A. Berle, president of the Audubon Society, "has jeopardized an already endangered sea turtle population [the Kemp's ridley]."

■ The verdict is still out on whether Gulf Coast shrimpers are in fact making use of TEDs, as well as whether the Bush administration will give in to shrimping industry interests.

■ An interim report by the National Academy of Sciences has determined that the Kemp's ridley is even more endangered than previously thought and that shrimp trawling is a significant cause of ridley mortality.

57–60 Four Simple Things You Can Do to Help

✔ **Don't buy or eat shrimp.** Both the National Audubon Society and the Reptile Defense Fund are urging people of good conscience to boycott shrimp. This long-standing boycott will end when shrimpers demonstrate that they are consistently in compliance with the law, and when law enforcement agents make TED enforcement a priority.

✔ **Ask your friends, family, and co-workers not to buy shrimp or products containing shrimp.** This includes pet food.

✔ **Please do not boycott restaurants serving shrimp, or groceries selling shrimp products.** It's the *shrimpers* who are the targets of this boycott, not *retailers*. You might want to explain to grocery and restaurant managers why they're selling less shrimp, and why the boycott continues.

✔ **If you wish to continue eating shellfish, try crayfish (crawfish) instead.** If you live in the North or the West, you can order crayfish through a seafood distributor or wholesaler. The price is about the same as that of shrimp, or slightly less, and many consumers prefer crayfish. You'll also be supporting the economy of states which shrimpers claim the boycott hurts.

The Good News

■ The U.S. Senate has passed a measure barring import of shrimp from nations whose shrimpers do not use Turtle Excluder Devices.

■ Volunteers and members of the Florida Panhandle Herpetological Society released 198 captive-hatched baby Loggerhead sea turtles as part of a volunteer turtle rescue project.

■ "Some species of sea turtle, such as the Kemp's ridley, nest only on very limited stretches of beach. When nesting females are threatened en route to that beach, or the beach itself is compromised by pollution or development, chances for successful nesting are slim. For years, biologists have excavated sea turtle nests, captive-hatched the babies, and released them on beaches far removed from their species' usual nesting site. The good news: adult specimens of these 'head-started' turtles seem to be returning to the *new* nesting site . . . a glimmer of hope for the turtles and a meaningful reward for the efforts of the many dedicated researchers, biologists, and volunteers who have worked hard to establish new nesting sites."*

THE MERCHANDISING OF EXTINCTION:
Elephants and the Ivory Trade

The African Wildlife Foundation reports:

The total elephant population of Africa was estimated at 1,300,000 in 1979. Today, fewer than 650,000 African elephants remain.

The volume of world trade in ivory from 1980 to 1985 was 800 tons each year.

To meet the yearly demand for 800 tons of ivory, some 90,000 elephants must be killed. Thousands of calves also die due to the loss of their mothers, bringing the estimated total up to 100,000 elephants a year.

The amount of illegal ivory circulating in the world market for the last several years is estimated by some experts to be over 90 percent.

The average tusk on the market weighed 21.3 pounds in 1982. Today, the average weight is 10 pounds, the size more common among adult female

*From Striking Back, *Reptile Defense Fund*

and young male elephants. As the animals with the largest tusks are being killed off, poachers are turning to younger animals with smaller tusks.

The world trade in unworked ivory amounts to nearly $50 million per year. Conservative estimates value the wholesale market of worked ivory at $500 million annually.

Prior to President Bush's June 5 [1989] ban on the importation of ivory into this country, the United States consumed $20–$30 million in raw and worked ivory each year. The U.S. and the European Community together accounted for 64 percent of the world's consumption of carved ivory. The United States imported in jewelry alone some 7.2 million pieces valued at $11.8 million annually.

Background

■ After a long battle, in October of 1989, the African elephant was listed on Appendix I of the Convention on International Trade in Endangered Species of Fauna and Flora (CITES). Appendix I lists endangered species that may become extinct if trade in them continues. Commercial trade in Appendix I species is prohibited.

■ It was also agreed that trade in ivory from elephants killed after February 1976 would be illegal (it was estimated at that time that 700 tons were stockpiled in Hong Kong).

■ In a compromise with several southern African countries (including South Africa) who want continuation of trade in ivory, it was agreed that a panel of experts will meet in 1992 to reconsider the issue. This panel will consider the possibility of "downlisting" the African elephant to Appendix II—in effect, reopening the ivory trade.

■ Zimbabwe, Botswana, Mozambique, Malawi, Burundi, and South Africa have stated point-blank that they will not abide by CITES' decision.

■ The U.S. Agency for International Development recently awarded Zimbabwe an $18 million grant for wildlife management policies that encourage controlled elephant hunting (i.e., "sport" hunting of elephants by rich Americans).

■ One pair of tusks can provide a poacher with the equivalent of one year's income.

■ Some in the fashion industry continue to glamorize the wearing of ivory. In the introductory campaign for a new Ralph Lauren cologne, "Safari," a full page ad in major fashion magazines featured a dressing table top carefully scattered with new ivory bracelets.

■ Times Square and Fifth Avenue trinket shops continue to sell ivory carved into kitschy sculptures. Some department stores continue to sell and promote ivory jewelry. Street vendors also persist in selling ivory jewelry.

■ Every five-and-a-half minutes another elephant is killed.

Three Simple Things You Can Do to Help　　61–63

✔ **Don't buy ivory.** Some stores still have ivory merchandise stockpiled. Don't buy it (that includes pianos with ivory keys). And don't wear the ivory jewelry you have now.

✔ **Ask your relatives who are traveling abroad,** especially those going to the Orient, not to buy ivory souvenirs or jewelry.

✔ **Ask local stores and catalogers** not to carry ivory jewelry or carvings.

And with Just a Little More Effort You Could . . .

✔ **Write to Ralph Lauren** and tell him that given the near-decimation of the African elephant for its ivory, and the international ban on trade in ivory, his approval of ads featuring ivory bracelets—instead of *live elephants*—to introduce a scent called "Safari" was exceptionally insensitive and inappropriate. Write to:

Mr. Ralph Lauren
550 Seventh Avenue
New York, NY 10020

✔ **In 1991**—the year before the CITES "panel of experts" will meet to consider reopening the ivory trade—start writing to President Bush and your congresspeople and senators, urging them to use their influence to keep the African elephant on Appendix I.

The Good News

■ Canada has banned all ivory imports.
■ Saks Fifth Avenue has discontinued all sales of ivory jewelry.

■ Cost Plus Imports of Oakland, CA, has also stopped all sales of ivory.

■ Sotheby's auction house was convinced by Friends of Animals to stop dealing in ivory.

■ Fashion industry giants Liz Claiborne, Ellen Tracy, Bill Blass, and Oscar de la Renta have made statements supporting a ban on all use of ivory.

■ Hecht's, Lord & Taylor, and R. H. Macy's have also endorsed a ban on ivory (the latter is currently being boycotted by Animal Rights Mobilization for its continuing sales of fur).

"YOUR CHILD OR YOUR DOG":
Experimental Use of Animals in Laboratories

• *According to Barnaby J. Feder, writing in* The New York Times, *estimates of the number of animals used each year in research laboratories vary from 10 million to 100 million. "Based on reports filed with the Department of Agriculture, the Congressional Office of Technology Assessment estimated that in 1983, the overall number was 'at least 17 million to 22 million.' "*

• *John McArdle, writing in* Animals' Agenda—*citing the volume mentioned by most animals rights groups—estimates that number as closer to 60 million animals.*

• *Experiments with animals cost taxpayers at least $4 billion a year.*

• *Many experiments have nothing to do with biomedical research. Other uses of laboratory animals include chemical warfare testing, nuclear radiation exposure, ballistic testing, animal addiction studies, and psychological experimentation.*

Background

■ The Animal Welfare Act does not cover rats, mice, farm animals, birds, and other species used in research—*as much as 90 percent of all animals used in research.*

■ Even in animals covered by the Act, it is up to the discretion of the researcher whether or not to administer anaesthesia or pain-relieving drugs.

■ Animals are kept in barren cages offering no stimulation or comfort, with little regard for species-specific needs.

■ Laboratories are rarely inspected. A report issued by the Office of Technology Assessment states that in 1983, 51.7 percent of the institutions in California and 48.7 percent in New York were not inspected at all.

■ The animal research industry is hugely profitable, supporting everything from multimillion-dollar construction programs to hazardous waste disposal companies.

■ Widespread belief in the value of animal research is continually reinforced by the academic community, where some of the most deeply entrenched and powerful academic scientists are animal researchers. These researchers write medical textbooks, teach medical students, edit professional journals, obtain millions of dollars in grant money—and intimidate or silence dissenters.

■ Physicians reevaluating medical history emphasize that key discoveries in the areas of heart disease, cancer, and diabetes have been made by clinical research, observation of patients, and human autopsies—not by animal experimentation.

■ According to the Medical Research Modernization Committee (MRMC): "The scientific tradition that medical hypotheses must be 'proven' in the lab has had unfortunate consequences. Frequently, effective therapies have been delayed because of the difficulty of finding an animal model that 'works.' For example, research with the animal model of polio resulted in a misunderstanding of the mechanism of infection. This delayed the development of the tissue culture, which was critical to the discovery of a vaccine."

■ On the subject of cancer, the MRMC states: "Misleading animal tests can be devastating for human health. For example, prior to 1963, all 27 prospective and retrospective studies of human patients showed a strong association between cigarette smoking and lung cancer. However, almost all efforts to cause lung cancer in laboratory animals failed. This delayed health warnings for years, and thousands of people subsequently died of cancer."

■ Billions of our tax dollars have been wasted on redundant, unnecessary, cruel experiments on animals. The "War on Cancer" alone, financed to the tune of one billion dollars a year, has cost American taxpayers untold sums of money and misery because of obsessive bioresearch emphasis on animal models. Harvard's Dr. John Bailar II, formerly the chief administrator of this effort, calls it a "qualified failure." John Leavitt of the Linus Pauling Institute says, "Only recently have we begun to realize the significance of [the] intuitive premise that human cancer, while fundamentally the same as rodent cancer, may have critical mechanistic differences which may in turn require different, uniquely human approaches to cancer eradication."

A PLEA FOR THE CHIMPS*
by Jane Goodall

Just after Christmas I watched, with shock, anger, and anguish, a videotape—made by an animal rights group during a raid—revealing the conditions in a large biomedical research laboratory, under contract to the National Institutes of Health, in which various primates, including chimpanzees, are maintained. In late March, I was given permission to visit the facility.

It was a visit I shall never forget. Room after room was lined with small bare cages, stacked one above the other, in which monkeys circled round and round and chimpanzees sat huddled, far gone in depression and despair.

Young chimpanzees, three or four years old, were crammed, two together, into tiny cages measuring 22 inches by 22 inches and only 24 inches high. They could hardly turn around. Not yet part of any experiment, they had been confined in these cages for more than three months.

The chimps had each other for comfort, but they would not remain together for long. Once they are infected, probably with hepatitis, they will be separated and each placed in another cage. And there they will remain, living in conditions of severe sensory deprivation, for the next several years. During that time, they will become insane.

A juvenile female rocked from side to side, sealed off from the outside world behind the glass doors of her metal isolation chamber. She was in semidarkness. All she could hear was the incessant roar of air rushing through vents into her prison . . .

I shall be forever haunted by her eyes, and by the eyes of the other infant chimpanzees I saw that day. Have you ever looked into the eyes of a person who, stressed beyond all endurance, has given up, succumbed utterly to the crippling helplessness of despair? I once saw a little African boy, whose whole family had been killed during the fighting in Burundi. He too looked out at the world, unseeing, from dull, blank eyes.

*Excerpted from "A Plea for the Chimps," by Jane Goodall, *New York Times Magazine*, May 17, 1987. Copyright © 1987 by The New York Times Company. Reprinted by permission.

"Biomedical researchers are not being defensive about using animals in medical research because animal models will save humanity (although they are indoctrinated to believe it). They're really defensive because animal models are indispensable to their ability to obtain grants. It's a scientific Catch-22 that is bleeding the lifeblood out of real medical progress."

—KENNETH P. STOLLER, M.D.

Just One Example of
How They're Wasting Your Money:
Drug Addiction Grants

While addicts have to wait six months to get into treatment programs, and the million and a half or more intravenous drug users menace all of us through muggings, burglaries, street violence—and transmission of AIDS to each other and their own babies—hundreds of millions of dollars are wasted each year on absurd drug experiments with animals. For example:

■ The Alcohol, Drug Abuse and Mental Health Administration (ADAMHA) spent $5,060,236 on a series of grants that financed turning macaque monkeys into addicts. The startling information to come out of the project: Monkeys become tolerant to different drugs at different rates, depending upon what drug they're using.

■ $839,276 was spent by ADAMHA to find out that, as Kenneth Stoller and Anne St. Laurent of United Action for Animals (UAA) phrased it, "given the choice between cocaine and/or amphetamines, hungry rats would rather have 'the real thing.'"

■ As reported by UAA, in a study financed by the Veterans Administration, researchers at the University of Arkansas learned that "purebred" pointers suffer more from the effects of morphine poisoning than do pointers specially bred to fear humans.

■ $740,000 paid for research at Johns Hopkins to find out that heroin-addicted baboons forced to choose between heroin and food will alternate their choices to get both.

■ $387,000 went to find out, at the University of South Carolina, that LSD given to cats causes shivering, erratic grooming, limb flicking, pouncing at imaginary objects, and continuous scratching.

■ $237,000 financed a study at the University of Maryland (Baltimore) to reveal that rabbits with nylon threads sewn through their eyelids, chained in stocks, electrically shocked, and given LSD, learn more quickly than do similar rabbits not given LSD.

■ Even prestigious Yale and Emory Universities have gotten into the act, with profitable ongoing drug addiction studies on animals.

For more information, send for a copy of: *Science Gone Insane,* United Action for Animals, 204 East 42 Street, New York, NY 10017; also, *A Critique of Animal Experiments on Cocaine Abuse,* New England Anti-Vivisection Society; and *The Case Book of Experiments with Living Animals,* American Anti-Vivisection Society, both at 801 Old York Road, Jenkintown, PA 19046.

Why Animal Research Persists*

Animal research is easy. It is simple to take a well-defined animal model, change a variable, and produce a paper for publication. This is a strong incentive in the "publish or perish" world of academia.

Animal research is fast. Human diseases generally span many years, but laboratory animals, with shorter lifespans, tend to have more rapidly progressive disease processes. This again facilitates quick, though often irrelevant, research.

Animal research is safe. It involves very little risk. Every experiment yields some data, which can then be compared to previous animal data as "new" and "interesting" findings.

Animal research is the "known." Many scientists are trained in and comfortable with animal research techniques. They are reluctant to adopt alternative methodologies, such as tissue cultures, which would require extensive retraining.

CHARITIES THAT FUND ANIMAL RESEARCH

When you plan your charitable contributions for the next year, you might want to take into consideration the fact that the following organizations fund research on animals. To determine the extent of animal testing used by each, as well as the purported purpose, ask your favorite health-related fund for their statistics on animal use. Tell them you won't give them any more money unless they disclose the information. Encourage them to use more non-animal alternatives—and, where possible, to devote a greater proportion of their budget to research on and public education about prevention.

American Cancer Society
American Diabetes Society
American Heart Association
American Kidney Fund
American Liver Foundation
American Lung Association
Arthritis Foundation
California Heart Association
Cystic Fibrosis Foundation
Easter Seals, Inc.
Epilepsy Foundation of America
Epstein-Barr Foundation

Fight for Sight, Inc.
Huntington's Disease Society of America
Incurably Ill for Animal Research
Leukemia Society of America
March of Dimes
Muscular Dystrophy Association
National Foundation for Ileitis and Colitis, Inc.
National Head Injury Foundation
National Kidney Foundation
National Multiple Sclerosis Society
United Cerebral Palsy Research and
    Educational Foundation

Courtesy of the Medical Research Modernization Committee

Animal research is flexible. Scientists can "prove" almost anything with animal models. Given the many species used and the nearly infinite number of variables that can be manipulated in animals, researchers can provide "scientific proof" of any theory they espouse. (Depending on the funding source, scientists have "proven" in animals that cigarettes cause cancer and that cigarettes do not cause cancer.)

Animal research is controllable. Scientists can control research variables much more tightly in animal experiments than is possible with human clinical research. The control, however, results in an unnatural and sometimes pathological setting for the animals, far from their natural habitat. The resulting stress influences the function of virtually every organ, and thus confounds the data.

Animal research is traditional. Whatever the reasons for this cultural phenomenon, the prestige accorded to animal research has important economic implications.

Animal research is readily funded. Funding agencies, reflecting the prestigious and familiar position of animal research in science, often favor these projects. Academic institutions, dependent on grant money for overhead expenses, often require that researchers secure most or all of their own salaries through grants. Consequently, the quest for funds becomes a primary motive, and the actual value of the research is a secondary concern.

"For more than a century the biomedical research community, its supporters and associated industries have attempted to portray the public's legitimate opposition to vivisection as some type of gladiatorial contest, depicting themselves as the true defenders of scientific advancement and protectors of our health and safety, and those who disagree with them as overly emotional, anti-science misanthropes. Such a simplistic distinction fails to consider the very serious ethical, medical, and scientific problems associated with the profligate use of experimental animals that characterizes the modern biomedical research establishment."

—JOHN McARDLE, *former animal researcher*

The Most Prolific Users of Laboratory Animals

The information below is from a report by The Investor Responsibility Research Center, based on data from the United States Department of Agriculture. The IRRC cautions that although rats and mice are said to constitute three-fourths or more of the experimental animals used in laboratories, the USDA does not collect data on either. Nor is there information available on the number of animals used by laboratories under contract to the corporations or universities mentioned below. Nevertheless, as incomplete as this information is, it is the best available.

Animals in the figures below are primarily: dogs, cats, rabbits, guinea pigs, monkeys, and other primates. Chimpanzees, an endangered species with physical and emotional needs much like our own, are included in the fugures as well; their continued use in research is one of the most egregious instances of animal abuse in laboratories. Goats, sheep, and pigs are included as well; these are primarily of interest to the military, for ballistics experiments, because of the fuss "do-gooders" make about the army's use of dogs for that purpose.

CORPORATIONS

American Cyanamid	55,460 animals
(includes 4,244 unrelievedly painful experiments)	
Rorer Group	39,984
Bayer	39,983
(includes 25,550 unrelievedly painful experiments)	
American Home Products	38,033
ICI Americas	34,065
Smith Kline Beckman	33,011
Merck	28,499
Johnson & Johnson	22,541
Schering-Plough	20,162

INSTITUTIONAL USERS

University of California (7 campuses)	76,698
University of Texas (all campuses)	33,253
Wilmington Medical Center	30,604
University of Southern California	25,116
University of Wisconsin	23,477
University of Illinois	19,111

The 153-page report, *Animal Testing and Consumer Products,* is available for $25 from: Investor Responsibility Research Center, 1755 Massachusetts Avenue, NW, Suite 600, Washington, DC 20036.

Alternatives to Animal Research*

Non-Invasive Imaging Techniques. The development of non-invasive imaging devices, such as CAT scans, MRI scans, and PET scans, have revolutionized clinical investigation. These technologies permit the ongoing evaluation of human diseases on human patients, rendering many uses of animals obsolete. For example, CAT and PET scans have been valuable for the study of parkinsonism, visual physiology, and musculoskeletal tumors.

Post-Market Surveillance. Thorough reporting of drug side effects by post-market surveillance is now possible, because the computer power needed to process the huge quantity of data is so inexpensive. Such a system would have identified the thalidomide disaster after only a few cases. When the first birth defects were noticed, however, scientists had great difficulty reproducing the deformities in laboratory animals, and it took several months before investigators could "prove" in animals that thalidomide causes birth defects.

Post-market surveillance would also increase the likelihood that unexpected, valuable uses of drugs would be recognized. Indeed, such serendipitous discoveries have led to many pharmaceutical advances, including anti-cancer medications such as prednisone, nitrogen mustard, and actinomycin D.

Autopsies. The autopsy rate in the United States has been falling steadily, much to the dismay of clinical investigators, who recognize the value of this traditional research tool. Autopsies have been critical to our current understanding of many diseases, such as diabetes and Alzheimer's disease.

Other Alternatives. *In vitro* cell and tissue cultures have strengths and limitations. They are not whole animals, and they may fail to reproduce interaction between organ systems. However, they can be powerful tools for studies at the cellular level, particularly when human tissues are used.

In the search for new anti-cancer drugs, 400,000 chemicals were screened, mostly on mice that were given leukemia. While a few compounds were effective against mouse leukemia, they had little, if any, effect against the major human killers. Today, this wasteful program is being replaced with a screen of about 100 human cancer cells *in vitro.* This alternative is

Courtesy of the Medical Research Modernization Committee

much less costly, and, because human cancers are being used, it should be more reliable.

Mathematical models, like *in vitro* models, are not perfect. However, these models can use human clinical data, and consequently the results may be more relevant to humans than conclusions based on animals.

The Good News

■ The last ten years have seen a substantial decline of laboratory animal use in the United States ranging from a one-time reported 100 percent use at several major cosmetics companies to roughly a 60 percent reduction at some major pharmaceutical companies.

■ A new scientific discipline of in vitro (non-animal) safety testing is growing rapidly with at least ten journals/newsletters devoted to alternative testing procedures.

■ The National Cancer Institute's new *in vitro* screen has reduced its use of animals from 6,000,000 to less than 300,000 per year.

■ Laboratory use of animals in Great Britain is down by 53 percent over the past decade.

■ Laboratory use of animals in the Netherlands is down by 23 percent during that same period.

■ As the result of a suit filed by the New England Anti-Vivisection Society, the Massachusetts Superior Court has ruled that animal care and use committees at the University of Massachusetts and its medical school must comply with the state's Open Meeting ("sunshine") Law. Committee meetings must be announced in advance and opened to the public.

■ Australia has adopted new ethics guidelines for experimenters, aimed at minimizing the number of experiments done using animals and eliminating any experiments that cause animals pain or distress. Project review committees will include an animal welfare worker and a member of the public.

■ Tufts University School of Veterinary Medicine now gives students the option of practicing their first surgeries on cadavers instead of live dogs.

■ Jerrold Tannenbaum, an ethics instructer at the Tufts veterinary school, recently published the first book written on veterinary ethics.

■ The City Council of Cambridge, MA, has unanimously voted in a new ordinance that permits inspection of privately-funded laboratories. The ordinance also establishes a position for a City Commissioner of Laboratory Animals; the new Commissioner is empowered to inspect facilities and other information relating to animal experimentation. Community groups or individuals interested in advancing similar ordinances can get more information by writing to: Cambridge Committee for Responsible Research, P.O. Box 1626, Cambridge, MA 02238.

■ Trans-Species Unlimited (now Animal Rights Mobilization) succeeded in closing down Cornell University Medical College's barbiturate addiction research on cats. The researcher involved returned $600,000 in federal grant monies.

■ The Letterman Institute of Army Research was pressured into returning 100 retired racing greyhounds to their former owners, who thought they had given the dogs up to be placed in homes. The Institute planned to use the dogs in bone injury experiments. According to the Physicians Committee for Responsible Medicine, who reviewed the protocols of the proposed experiment, the studies could easily have been done in conjunction with a veterinary school since naturally-occurring fractures in dogs are common in veterinary practice.

■ The Eli Lilly Company has used recombinant DNA technology from non-animal sources to produce a human insulin analog, Nucellin, equal to glandular insulin in potency. For information: Elanco, Biotech Sales, Lilly Corporation Center, Indianapolis, IN 46285, (317) 276-3000.

Four Simple Things You Can Do to Help   64–67

✔ **Attend the Annual AFAAR Walkathon for Laboratory Animals.** Held in New York City the first week of May. Have fun and do good. Contact: American Fund for Alternatives to Animal Research, 175 West 12 Street, 16-G, New York, NY 10011, (212) 242-0390.

✔ **Participate in World Laboratory Animal Liberation Week activities** in late April. You can find out about events all over the country by contacting: In Defense of Animals, 21 Tamal Vista Boulevard, Corte Madera, CA 94925 (415) 924-4454.

✔ **Try not to use any unnecessary prescription or over-the-counter drugs.** It just contributes to the development of even more unnecessary drugs (how many different analgesics do we need?)—and tortures more animals.

✔ **If you work in a laboratory,** report violations of the Animal Welfare Act to: Legal Action for Animals, 205 East 42 Street, New York, NY 10017. LAA is also looking for people who will post their notices on key university bulletin boards.

And with Just a Little More Effort You Could . . .

✔ **Help stop redundant animal experiments,** by asking your senators and congresspersons to back Representative Robert Torricelli's (D-NJ) annual attempt to start a National Center for Research Accountability (H.R. 560—The Research Accountability Act). The Center would conduct full text literature searches of all project proposals involving live animals before funding is granted. The Act also requires the National Library of Medicine to develop systems capable of disseminating the results of all current biomedical research to medical libraries. The Congressional Budget Office estimates that implementation would cost $38 million; we're wasting at least that much on redundant experiments each year.

✔ **Be a human testing volunteer,** instead of animals. Contact: Humans for Alternative Research and Testing, Box 8756, Greenville, SC 29604.

✔ **If you are a mental health professional, M.D., drug counselor, or ex-addict,** and are willing to speak out against drug addiction studies involving animals, contact: Betsy Swart, International Society for Animal Rights, 421 South State Street, Clarks Summit, PA 18411, (717) 586-2200.

✔ **Help save the last chimpanzees on earth** by stopping their use in medical experimentation. Contact your members of Congress and ask them to cut off funding for *all* experiments involving chimpanzees, including controversial AIDS research on chimpanzees.

✔ **Stop cruel animal testing at universities.** There are several letter-writing campaigns going on right now, sponsored by various animal rights organizations (if you'd like more information about each situation, write to the sponsoring animal rights organizations mentioned below.

Yale University. Ask them to stop wasteful drug addiction experiments on animals and help the humans desperately in need of rehabilitation. Letter-writing campaign sponsored by In Defense of Animals. Write to:

Benno Schmidt
President
Yale University
1302-A Yale Station
New Haven, CT 06520

Emory University. Ask them to stop Dr. Larry Byrd's wasteful drug addiction experiments on chimpanzees and squirrel monkeys. Sponsored by In Defense of Animals. Write to:

James Laney
President
Emory University
Atlanta, GA 30322

University of North Carolina. Ask them to stop cruel and stressful experiments being conducted on cats and kittens at the Greensboro campus. Sponsored by North Carolina Network for Animals. Write:

William E. Moran
Chancellor
University of North Carolina—Greensboro
303 Mossman Building
Greensboro, NC 27412

Louisiana State University. Ask the Secretary of Defense to stop the $2.1 million "redundant, scientifically flawed and ethically unacceptable" ballistic wound experiments at LSU Medical School by Dr. Michael Carey. The cats receive no post-injury pain relief. Letter campaign sponsored by Physicians Committee for Responsible Medicine. Call or write:

Richard Cheney
Secretary of Defense
Room 3EE880
Pentagon
Washington, DC 20301

Honorable Les Aspin
Chairman
House Armed Services
   Committee
Washington, DC 20515
(202) 225-4151

Honorable Sam Nunn
Chairman
Senate Armed Services
   Committee
Washington, DC 20510
(202) 224-3871

University of Pennsylvania. Protest U.P. School of Veterinary Medicine researcher Adrian Morrison's notorious experiments on cats. For updated information and demonstration schedule, contact: National Association of Nurses Against Vivisection, P.O. Box 42110, Washington, DC 20015 (301) 770-7444.

✔ **Contact those companies whose products you use** (you can check the product containers for company names; call to obtain the name of the chief executive officer [CEO] and address [usually it's not on the product]) and tell them that you know that some other companies have substantially reduced their use of animals. Ask what they are doing. Remember: Direct consumer pressure can and does have enormous impact.

Dear {name of CEO}:

A number of leading corporations have recently engaged in successful efforts to reduce animal use and suffering. As an animal protectionist and a consumer of your product {name it}, I am writing to you for information on your company's efforts in this area.

Has your company developed a plan to promote and implement alternatives? If you have developed such a plan, please attach a copy of it. If not, do you plan to develop and implement one? When?

What specific actions has your company taken to phase down and phase out animal use and to minimize animal pain and suffering in your own and in contract labs? What has been the result of these efforts?

If your company provides financial and/or technical support for any alternative programs, please indicate what they are and the amount of support.

Thank you for your consideration.

Sincerely,

Anna Sequoia

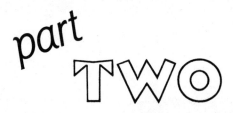

part
TWO

"We are the generation that searched on Mars for evidence of life but couldn't rouse enough moral sense to stop the destruction of even the grandest manifestations of life on earth. In that sense we are like the Romans whose works of art, architecture and engineering inspire our awe but whose traffic in slaves and gladiatorial combat is mystifying and loathsome."

—*DR. ROGER PAYNE, noted whale conservationist*

MAIL ORDER SOURCES:
Cosmetics and Household Products
Not Tested on Animals

Because it may be difficult, even if you live in a big city, to locate commonly used items like hair colorings, nail polish remover, and wool wash that have not been tested on animals, we include the following mail order guide. Try to plan ahead, so that you won't suddenly run out of dishwashing liquid or sun block cream, and impulsively buy a brand that perpetuates cruelty to animals or to the environment.

You'll notice that we've kept an eye open for value. Some not-tested-on-animals products are more expensive than you might be used to. But there are tremendous bargains, too, and those are noted.

Most of the mail order sources listed accept payment by Visa or MasterCard. To the best of our knowledge, none accepts American Express. Despite repeated protests from people who care about animals, American Express continues to feature furs in their catalogs and bill inserts. Most catalogers request that you include $1 for each catalog.

The prices and products noted below are based on catalogs surveyed in April 1990 and are subject to change.

Alexandra Avery Purely Natural Body Care
Northrup Creek
Clatskanie, OR 97016
(503) 755-2446

Alexandra Avery is a small company still handpicking and processing most of its own herbal and floral materials from its own gardens. The skin care line has no synthetic preservatives, scents, colorings, or fillers like stearic acid. They offer several sampler and gift sets, including a sampler of four different perfumes, $6 plus $2.50 shipping; and a body care sampler consisting of a full-size soap, 1 oz. toner, body oil, lip balm, and perfume, all for $10 plus $2.50 shipping. While Alexandra Avery does not sell conventional "war paint" (lipstick, mascara, etc.), it has a nice, exceptionally inexpensive moisturizer to go under your makeup: Almond Cream, $11 for 2 ounces. They have wonderful body powder too, massage oils, hair oil (for hot oil treatments), and more. All essential oils are from cruelty-free labs. No animal ingredients.

Amberwood
Route 1, Box 206
Milner, GA 30257
(404) 358-2991

Amberwood is a very good, broad-range catalog of both personal care and household care products. Part of the profits from the catalog go into educational programs directed toward publicizing/remedying the problems of wild burros. They have just about anything you might need for your toilette: toothpaste, lip balm, moisturizer, foot lotion, dusting powder, suntan lotion, shaving cream, henna hair coloring, shampoo, and more. They carry Paul Penders, Beauty Without Cruelty and Viva Vera cosmetics, all moderately priced. Samples of most makeup foundation shades are available and cost 50¢ each. Household products range from Golden Lotus fabric softener to Ecover toilet cleaner. Everything in this catalog is made without animal ingredients.

Bare Escentuals
104 Cooper Court
Los Gatos, CA 95030
In California: (800) 227-3788
All other calls: (800) 227-3386

Bare Escentuals has several retail stores in California, but it sells by mail and phone too. Their cosmetics color choices are incredible: in mascara alone, you can choose from teal, purple, navy blue, emerald green, electric blue, browns, and black. They have 35 different eyeshadows. They also carry rice powder—generally, not that easy to find—as well as facial masks and scrubs, bath crystals, and skin lotions. A full ingredient list for each item is sent along with the mail order materials. Prices are fair, not cheap, but lower than most premium department store tested-on-animals brands.

Basically Natural
109 East G Street
Brunswick, MD 21716
(301) 834-7923

Basically Natural offers cosmetics and household products from England, Ireland, Scotland, Holland, Germany, Australia, India, as well as the U.S. Most of their products are vegan, that is, containing no animal ingredients of any kind. The balance may contain substances such as beeswax, honey, or lanolin, but these items are clearly marked. Interestingly, if you're not sure what color makeup to order, you can send them a color sample to match. In addition to a fair range of cosmetics, Basically Natural has some specialty products you may want to try, such as all natural Citrus II™ air freshener that comes in a non-aerosol bottle; Faith Products' Faith in Nature vegetable oil soap that is reputed to be the best-selling cruelty-free soap in Scotland; and Green Ban plant extract insect repellents for people, plants, or companion animals.

Baubiologie Hardware
207B 16th Street
Pacific Grove, CA 93950
(408) 372-8626

This is a fantastic catalog. Products range from Granny's Power Plus Laundry Concentrate (one tablespoonful will clean an average load; this may be the most economical laundry concentrate available anywhere), to Radon air sampler kits. There are *many* products included here that you won't find in other catalogs. Here's just a small sample: AFM [wax] Stripper 66; AFM Spackling Compound; AFM Safecoat Semi Gloss Enamel, with no heavy metal compounds like lead, mercury, arsenic; AFM Safecoat Water Based Wood Stain; AFM Wallpaper Adhesive. They also carry computer paper that is made of 50 percent recycled paper. And ladybugs by the quart to control the aphids, leafhoppers, mites, and mealy bugs in your garden. The AFM products in the catalog (and there are many you'll want if you are about to redecorate your apartment or office or if you simply own your own home), are tested using the EYTEX™ ocular safety test. This test does not use animals.

Beauty Naturally®
57 Bosque Road, P.O. Box 429
Fairfax, CA 94930
(415) 459-2826

Beauty Naturally carries Vita Wave's hard-to-find, not-tested-on-animals hair coloring products. Be sure to order them well before your roots are showing; Vita Wave is a small company and sometimes has a difficult time keeping up with demand, so there may be a wait for them. But if you color your hair, their products are worth the necessary planning. The colorings contain no peroxide or harsh chemical dyes, and the home permanents contain no thioglycolic acid.

Beauty Naturally also carries an interesting line of skin care products for men and women. Its eye cream is $22.50 for 5 ounces—about one-fourth to one-fifth the price of similar department store animal-tested brands. Its

Bagno de Mare, a foaming gel for shower or bath, sounds delicious; it includes peach oil, scented by a touch of vanilla.

The Body Shop
1341 Seventh Street
Berkeley, CA 94710   (415) 524-0360

This isn't the Body Shop you've seen on Madison Avenue and in *The New York Times*. In fact, this Body Shop was opened in Berkeley in 1970, and from the first offered its lotions and potions in refillable containers (the other Body Shop opened in England in 1976). In 1987, when the British company wanted to open retail outlets here, they bought the rights in this country to this Body Shop's name—and our own American Body Shop now operates under license to them. Get it? No matter . . .

This Body Shop offers a splendid array of not-tested-on-animals products, including sixteen scented glycerine soap bars with names that range from Black Poppy, China Rain, and Venom, to the more prosaic Patchouli, Almond, and Rose. Their Shaving Gel is a good alternative to "beard-busting" (and environment- and animal-busting) Barbasol. Their Extra Rich Night Cream is astoundingly inexpensive: two ounces for under $5. And they pay shipping costs.

One of the most fascinating services this Body Shop offers is that they will custom-scent your aftershave, bubble bath, skin lotion, dusting powder, as well as other products, with the essential perfume oils you choose. The charge for this service is well under $1 per product. This Body Shop offers no conventional makeup.

The Body Shop
45 Horsehair Road
Hanover Technical Center
Cedar Knolls, NJ 07927-2003
To order a catalog: (800) 541-2535

This is the Body Shop everyone knows about and which has taken the concept of not-tested-on-animals cosmetics out into the mainstream of American life. Their retail shops are attractive, enticing, with high prices for some items, but extremely reasonable prices for others. It does have an amazing range of products, many of which contain no animal ingredients (ask to see their ingredients book if you're looking for vegan products). Friends who color their hair recommend Body Shop's Protein Cream Rinse (8.4 oz. for $8.40). We've used their Moisture Cream with Vitamin E—a bargain, compared to Shiseido or Prescriptives, say, at $8.35. Their under-eye concealer is excellent, and a buy at $3.75. Beyond that, The Body Shop has a lot to please you: shaving cream, soaps, scents, eye definers, lipsticks in good colors, and much more.

Borlind of Germany
Otterville Road—P.O. Box 1487
New London, NH 03257
(603) 526-2076 in New Hampshire
(800) 447-7024

Borlind of Germany is one of the most popular natural skin care lines
in Europe. Prices are by no means cheap ($25 for a liquid makeup base,
$15 for eyeshadow, $10.50 for lipstick), but the colors are subtle, sophisticated—and the range of nail colors is one of the best produced by a cosmetics manufacturer specializing in not-tested-on-animals products. There's
nothing "health-foody" about these cosmetics at all; this is the mail order
material to order if you prefer a high-fashion look.

Borlind's other products include baby shampoo, baby cleansing milk,
eye wrinkle cream, sun block, and under-eye cover sticks. They offer trial
sizes of many of their products, including the eye wrinkle cream, décolleté
cream, and baby products, most for under $2 each. When you write, ask
for their trial size order form.

The Compassionate Consumer
P.O. Box 27
Jericho, NY 11753
(718) 445-4134

The Compassionate Consumer's catalog—and range of merchandise—is
one of the most comprehensive available. It includes products from manufacturers like Paul Penders, Aubrey Organics, Weleda, and Warm Earth
Cosmetics. They have a nice choice of fragrances for men and women, as
well as skin cleaners and toners, moisturizers, and body creams. Their Orjene Cosmetics Kelp Sea Protein Shampoo is considerably less expensive
than most not-tested-on-animals shampoos available from health food stores
or via mail order (16 ounces, under $5). The Compassionate Consumer also
carries Vita Wave's perms and hair color.

Other not-tested-on-animals products include: dental floss, mouthwash,
sun block, deodorant, baby lotion, baby shampoo, organic dog shampoo,
vegan dog biscuits, and herbal flea collars for dogs or cats. Their selection
of household products ranges from laundry detergent, to automatic dishwasher powder, to biodegradable bleach. Vegans may be interested in their
non-leather athletic shoes, acupressure sandals, and boat/deck shoes.

Ecco Bella
6 Provost Square (Suite 602)
Caldwell, NJ 07006
(201) 226-5799

Ecco Bella produces one of the few big four-color catalogs we've seen for not-tested-on-animals products. They offer a better variety of household cleaners than almost anyone: Ecover floor soap, cream cleaner (for tile, acrylic, and fiberglass surfaces), wool wash (cheaper than Woolite); Ecco Bella all-natural orange all-purpose cleaner; non-aerosol air freshener; biodegradable food storage bags; cotton coffee filters; cedar "mothballs"; liquid enzyme drain cleanser; laundry "booster and whitener"; fabric softener; and wooden veggie and jar brushes with vegetable fiber bristles.

For companion animals, Ecco Bella has Green Ban dog shampoo; Nature's Miracle stain and odor remover; Pow Herbal Flea Powder; and nutritional yeast and garlic bits. For the animals' people, they offer cleansing grains, bath salts, and body powders, packaged in small, biodegradable bags (use your own dispenser or buy their refillable ones). In addition to a full line of Aubrey Organics men's skin care items (ginseng face scrub, face cream, shaving cream, aftershave), there are more colors of cosmetics here than you'll ever require in a lifetime. The Barry M cosmetics are very theatrical: bright yellow and bright red eye shadows; intense violet mascara or hair streakers; eyeliner in glossy copper; "dazzle dust" in jarring shades of royal blue, hot pink, and orange. You can choose more subtle shades too (they're here)—but this is the place to shop for flash.

Ecco Bella has Vita Wave hair products too, plus a variety of other products: shampoo, dental floss; recycled paper products; some natural gourmet foods (saffron pasta, for example, or pesto herbal mix); and organically grown coffee.

Eco-Choice

P.O. Box 281
Montvale, NJ 07645-0281
(201) 930-9046 in New Jersey
(800) 535-6304

If you've been searching for a not-tested-on-animals nail polish remover, you can get what you need here. DeLore Nail Polish Remover is also formaldehyde- and acetone-free. Eco-Choice also carries professional quality Giovanni hair aids you may have trouble locating in not-tested-on-animals versions: Jazz Brilliantine, for a high-shine dressing for spiking and wisping hair; and L.A. Grab Extra Hold Finishing Spray. They carry Biotene H-24 Dandruff Shampoo too.

This is the right catalog, too, if you've been trying to locate a not-tested-on-animals furniture or floor polish. In the one-quart size, AFM All Purpose Polish and Wax should do you for the next couple years (or combine your order with a friend and divide the contents of the bottle). A quart of Ecover

Wool Wash will last a good long time too (and it's so much cheaper than Woolite).

Eco-Choice also offers Annemarie Borlind cosmetics; sun block creams; face care preparations; Camocare throat spray and gargle; Vegalatum, a non-petroleum-based jelly; baby powder; carpet shampoo; energy-saving light bulbs; and toilet paper made from 100% recycled paper. Order the brochure by phone free, or send $2 for a catalog, brochure, and free sample.

Humane Alternative Products
8 Hutchins Street
Concord, NH 03301
(603) 224-1361

This is an excellent general catalog, with a wide range of products. You'll find: Vita Wave non-toxic permanent wave kits, as well as Vita Wave hair colors; No Common Scents liquid insect repeller; Aubrey Organics organic pet shampoo; Weleda non-aerosol spray deodorant; men's ginseng shaving cream; soaps; colognes; Paul Penders lipsticks, blushers, mascara; Allen's Naturally dishwasher compound; and more. Their unpretentious catalog even contains a selection of cruelty-free office supplies by International Rotex, including Bond White Correction Fluid—a nice substitute for the tested-on-animals correction fluids found in most offices. All of the products in this catalog contain no animal ingredients.

Lion and Lamb Cruelty-Free Products, Inc.
29–28 41st Avenue (Suite 813)
Long Island City, NY 11101
(718) 361-5757

This sixteen-page catalog contains a broad selection of products: Rainbow, Abracadabra, and Bellmira bubble baths; Alba Botanical, Orjene, and Earth Science shaving creams; Kiss My Face cleansers, moisturizers, citrus astringent; Earth Science mousse and hairspray; DeLore nail polish remover; Kappus fruit soaps; Naturade dandruff shampoo; and Nature's Gate baby shampoo. They have a good selection too of household cleaning products: non-chlorine liquid bleach; laundry detergent; furniture polish in a carbon dioxide–powered aerosol; glass cleaner. If you're interested in cosmetics, ask to see their new color cosmetics catalog. Lion & Lamb has samples and testers available for most of the products in their catalog; these cost less than $1 each. Fifteen percent of Lion & Lamb's profits are donated to animal rights and wildlife preservation organizations.

Pamela Marsen, Inc.
Beauty Without Cruelty, Ltd.
451 Queen Anne Road
Teaneck, NJ 07666
(201) 836-7820

Beauty Without Cruelty has been in business more than 20 years. Right from the start, this United Kingdom–based company used long established, safe ingredients and promised not to test products on animals. Several of their products do contain lanolin or beeswax, but many more contain no animal ingredient whatsoever. BWC's color range is extremely good, with 21 different lipsticks, several with matching nail enamel, 6 different lip color crayons, and 19 different eyeshadows. The lipsticks are unperfumed and contain PABA, the sunscreen. The water-based foundation is unperfumed as well, as in fact are all their cosmetics. BWC also offers suntan lotions, moisturizers, henna hair treatments, fragrances for men and women, soap, deodorant, shampoos, and hand lotion. Prices are extremely reasonable.

Naturally Ewe
2411 Devonwoode Place
Seffner, FL 33584
(813)-681-6787

Naturally Ewe carries a wide selection of Paul Penders cosmetics and body care products. Paul Penders's colors are, for the most part, soft and natural-looking. The makeup cream (foundation) has good coverage, but a light texture.

This well-thought-of line includes skin toners, moisturizers, night cream, beauty mask, shampoo, conditioner, body lotion, and shave cream. Prices are generally quite good, and Naturally Ewe sometimes includes $1-off coupons with its information sheets.

No Common Scents
Kings Yard
220 Xenia Avenue
Yellow Springs, OH 45387
(513) 767-4261 (OH, IN, IL, MI, WI)   (800) 686-0012 (others)

No Common Scents has a vast selection of essential oils, which can be used alone or blended to scent the body (or buy one of their inexpensive light rings, which can be used to scent the home). Their prices are excellent. They do have glycerine soap too, and moisture lotions that they will scent for you. Amazingly, while nothing else in No Common Scents' product list contains animal ingredients or is tested on animals, the gelatin capsules they sell come from *whale fat*. Totally disgusting—and inexcusable.

People for the Ethical Treatment of Animals
P.O. Box 42516
Washington, DC 20015-0516
(800) 673-8501

PETA offers a few basic household products by Allen's Naturally and offers discounts of approximately 10 percent for PETA members (ask to see a copy of their gift catalog). Products include dishwashing liquid, automatic dishwashing detergent, liquid laundry detergent, and no-phosphate fabric softener. This is a good place to buy your basics, as all the profits go toward supporting the organization's work.

Rainbow Research Corporation
170 Wilbur Place
Bohemia, NY 11716
(516) 589-5563   (800) 589-5563 (outside NY)

If you need henna, this is the place, with 12 different shades. Rainbow is also a very good source for scented bubble bath in reasonably large quantities (16 ounces), for reasonably low prices (under $5). People with sensitive skin now using Aveeno soap may want to try Rainbow's Aloe/Oatmeal bar. Products contain no animal ingredients, except for their Rainbow Golden Oil, which contains lanolin.

Yvonne Richards, Ltd.
P.O. Box 476
Whitehouse, NJ 08888

Yvonne Richards is an excellent source of personal and household care products. They also carry Paul Penders cosmetics, though you'll have to know these to order properly; the catalog offers no real help in color selection. But they are particularly strong in the area of body care, moisturizers, scrubs, and powders, ranging from Autumn Harp Body Lotion with Aloe Vera and Rose, to Weleda's Citrus Body Oil. Richards also carries several hard-to-find DeLore nail care products: formaldehyde-free Nail Protector; Nail Fix, an adhesive gel that repairs broken, split, or cracked nails; Chip Proof Polish Shield; Organic Nail Hardener; and, of course, they carry DeLore acetone-free Unique Polish Remover.

Companion animals fare well in this catalog, with EcoSafe's Herbal Shampoo & Dip for Dogs, and Lightening Products' non-toxic Organic Cat Shampoo, for relief of biting, licking, and scratching caused by fleas. The range of household products is excellent, with all the basics (Ecover Laundry Powder; Ecover Wool Wash; Allen's Naturally Dishwashing Liquid), plus some items not commonly listed in catalogs: Magic American's Furniture Magic, an environmentally-safe aerosol polish-cleaner, for example, and Magic American's Tile 'n Grout Magic, also in an aerosol. Yvonne Richards will order household soaps and cleaners in larger sizes for people with large homes or families or a compulsion to clean.

Seventh Generation
Colchester, VT 05446-1672
(800)456-1177

In addition to a standard selection of non-tested-on-animals household cleaners, Seventh Generation offers paper towels, tissues, and toilet tissue of recycled paper, sold by the case; computer paper of recycled paper; radon detectors—and a lot more.

Sombra
5600-G McLeod Street NE
Albuquerque, NM 87109
(505) 888-0288
(800) 225-3963

People with allergies may be particularly interested in Sombra's foundation makeup. It's made without preservatives, nor, its manufacturer claims, is it subject to bacterial decomposition or contamination. The foundation is also made without solvents or dilutants, so it's quite economical. Sombra's blushers are made without preservatives either, and like the foundation contain no animal ingredients. Sombra also produces an extremely appealing line of skin, body, and hair care products, including Cherry Almond Moisturizing Hair Conditioner, Oats & Honey Facial Scrub, Lemon Skin Freshener, and Pineapple Cocoanut Hand & Body Lotion.

Spare the Animals Cruelty-Free Products
P.O. Box 233
Tiverton, RI 02878
(401) 625-5963

Spare the Animals offers several brands of products not included in other mail order catalogs we've seen. For example, in the category of household products, they have Life Tree Premium Laundry Liquid and Life Tree Premium Dishwashing Liquid. They also carry Nettlerose Shampoo with Herbal Conditioners, and Herbal Renewal Shampoo and Conditioner, both particularly good for dry or damaged hair. For children, they have Earthchild

Baby Oil with Calendula, containing no petroleum derivatives, chemical preservatives, or synthetic fragrances or colors.

One of the best things about this catalog is that Spare the Animals lists the ingredients of each product, something allergy sufferers will appreciate. The selection here is not huge, but this purveyor offers an excellent group of products. Their attitude is good too: they use no plastic packing materials, unless these have been used to pack something sent to them; they reuse shipping cartons and paper packing materials; and none of their products contains animal ingredients.

Vegan Street
P.O. Box 5525
Rockville, MD 20855
(800) 422-5525

Vegan Street is an all-purpose catalog with some interesting products. It has the usual (and necessary) laundry detergent and dishwashing liquid. But it also has: Superglue, household cement for mending china, glass, wood, and metal; and E-Z On shoe polish. They're one of the few catalogers to carry Giovanni hair care products, including Giovanni's Dash of L.A. for spiking your hair. There are some other not-so-easy-to-find, useful products too, such as pure cocoanut oil, which is nice to apply to your skin right after a bath. This is one of the few catalogs to feature Vegedog, a supplement that will enable your dog to healthfully join you in your vegetarian or vegan diet. Vegan Street will also help chemically sensitive people locate appropriate products to use.

Weleda, Inc.
841 South Main Street
Spring Valley, NY 10977
(914) 356-4134

The Weleda company is based on Anthroposophy, a spiritual/scientific movement founded at the beginning of the century by Rudolph Steiner. According to Weleda's literature, they believe that "although human beings have gradually withdrawn from nature, they are still nourished, healed and refreshed by its forces." They therefore use no synthetic preservatives or artificial coloring or cosmetic agents, nor do they test on animals. Their products are pleasant to use. The Iris Cleansing Lotion, for example, has a pleasant, citrusy scent and creates a tingling feeling as it is applied to the skin. Other products include: Iris night cream, soap, moisturizing cream; Rosemary shampoo, conditioner; Natural Salt Toothpaste; Citrus Body Oil; Natural Sage Deodorant. They're now also selling some interesting homeopathic medicines.

MAKE IT YOURSELF:
Homemade Household Product Recipes

Every time you can substitute a cleaning or personal hygiene product you make yourself for the invariably polluting and/or caustic products we're used to buying in the supermarket, you're achieving several goals. First of all, you save money. That alone isn't such a bad thing; use it well. But you'll also help preserve the environment—and in the process spare scores of animals needless suffering.*

Cleansers

Wine/Coffee Stains Blot the fresh spill with a cloth soaked with club soda.

Cooking Utensils Let pots and pans soak in a baking soda solution before washing.

Copper Use a paste of lemon juice, salt, and flour; or rub vinegar and salt into the copper.

Furniture Polish Mix three parts olive oil and one part vinegar, or one part lemon juice and two parts olive oil. Use a soft cloth.

General Cleaner Mix baking soda with a small amount of water.

Glassware White vinegar or rubbing alcohol and water.

Headlights, Mirrors, Windshields Wipe with a damp cloth or sponge sprinkled with baking soda. Rinse with water and dry with a soft towel.

Household Cleaner Three tablespoons baking soda mixed into one quart warm water.

Linoleum Floors One cup of white vinegar mixed with two gallons of water to wash, club soda to polish.

Microwave Ovens Clean and deodorize the insides of the oven and around the door seal with a baking soda solution. For stubborn odors, leave an open box of baking soda inside, but be sure to remove it before each use.

Mildew Remover Lemon juice or white vinegar and salt.

Oil and Grease on Driveway Remove by sprinkling the area with kitty litter, allow it to absorb, then remove it with a shovel or broom.

*Courtesy of People for the Ethical Treatment of Animals

Oil Stains White chalk rubbed into the stain before laundering.

Porcelain Dip damp cloth in baking soda and rub over stains. For especially stained surfaces, make a paste with water and apply it. Allow to set before rubbing clean and rinsing.

Silverware Polish To remove tarnish, apply a baking soda paste with a damp sponge or soft cloth. Rub until clean and buff to a shiny gloss.

General Stains and Toilet Bowls Vinegar.

Stainless Steel Polish Baking soda or mineral oil to shine; vinegar to remove spots.

Insect Repellents

Ants Pour a line of cream of tartar at the place where ants enter the house—they will not cross it.

Wash countertops, cabinets, and floors with equal parts vinegar and water.

Caterpillars Stripping old fruit from the vines and trees will keep insects from laying eggs.

Cockroaches Place whole bay leaves in several locations around kitchen.

Fleas and Ticks Feed brewer's yeast, vitamin B, and garlic tablets to companion animals. Place herbs such as fennel, rue, pennyroyal and rosemary and/or eucalyptus seeds and leaves where the animal sleeps or on the animal to repel fleas.

Mosquitoes Eat brewer's yeast or take it in tablet form daily during the summer months.

Mothballs Place cedar chips around clothes; dried lavender can be made into sachets and placed in drawers and closets.

Personal Hygiene

Deodorant Dust underarms with a little baking soda.

Mouthwash One teaspoon of baking soda dissolved in half a glass of water.

Sunburn Soak in a baking soda bath or apply a damp cloth saturated with a baking soda solution; or spray sunburn with vinegar.

Toothpaste Mix together three parts baking soda and one part water. (Only to be used by adults. Baking soda does not contain fluoride, which is important for children's teeth.)

NOTE: Some vinegar may be filtered through gelatin, which comes from animal by-products. You may want to use unfiltered vinegar.

ADOPT-AN-ANIMAL PROGRAMS:
In Which They Keep the Animals

Farm Sanctuary
Adopt A Farm Animal Project
P.O. Box 150
Watkins Glen, NY 14891
(607) 583-2225

Every month, Farm Sanctuary adoption workers rescue animals from factory farms, slaughterhouses, confinement operations, stockyards, and "livestock" auctions throughout the country. Frequently, rescued animals have been abused or abandoned. For example, current residents include a veal calf, now named Alby, who was chained to his crate and left to starve to death on a Pennsylvania farm, and a pig, now called Hope, who was left, with an injured leg, to die a slow death at a stockyard. To these and other animals, Farm Sanctuary workers are angels of mercy—and well deserve as much help as you can possibly give them.

For reasonable fees, you can adopt a variety of animals: $20 a month will support a pig; a chicken will cost $6 a month; a rabbit, $8; adopting a cow runs $40 a month; a turkey, $10; a goat, $20; a duck, $8; a goose, $10. A good idea is to share the cost with an animal-loving friend or co-worker. Monthly sponsors receive a framed color photograph of the animal or animals they adopt, as well as regular progress reports.

Each Thanksgiving, Farm Sanctuary puts particular emphasis on their Adopt-A-Turkey program (the theme is, obviously, adopt one—don't eat one). This would make a fabulous activity for an elementary school class. It could even include a trip to Farm Sanctuary to visit the turkey, or whatever other animals the class adopts.

Farm Sanctuary also runs an active out-placement adoption service for former factory-farm animals.

The Fund for Animals
200 West 57 Street
New York, NY 10019
(212) 246-2096   (212) 246-2632

The Fund for Animals' new Foster Parent Program was started because the Fund has more animals under its permanent protection than any other humane society. Most of the animals, including thousands of wild burros it has rescued from Grand Canyon and Death Valley (and the Bureau of Land Management), do find permanent homes. But others, including the lame or the blind, remain at one of their three permanent facilities. One current resident at Black Beauty Ranch, in Murchison, TX, is Nim, the famous chimpanzee, the first to learn sign language and communicate with humans. Nim, who had been raised in a house with a human family, and who had been featured in *Life* and other magazines, had outlived the sign language experiment itself. With a degree of mercilessness that is impossible to fathom, Nim had been sent off to a laboratory where—until rescued by Fund for Animals' president, Cleveland Amory—the first chimpanzee to speak with humans was about to be used in invasive medical research.

The Fund's Animal Trust Sanctuary and Wildlife Rehab Center in Ramona, California, houses a few of the many goats it saved from San Clemente Island, many cats and dogs (some of the latter from laboratories), and a variety of sparrow hawks, barn owls, opossums, and other critters. Their Rabbit Sanctuary in Simpsonville, SC, houses hundreds of rabbits rescued from commercial breeders, pet stores, and laboratories. To become a Fund for Animals Foster Parent, the maintenance is $42 to support one rabbit for one year. To become a sponsor of another animal in the Fund's care, please call them at the numbers indicated above.

Orphan Alley
N 2658 C.T.A.
Gresham, WI 54128
(715) 787-4265

For as little as $10, you can "adopt" a cat or kitten that will remain at this shelter. Volunteers at the shelter will send you a photograph of and letter about the animal chosen for you.

Save the Manatee Club
Adopt-a-Manatee Program
500 N. Maitland Avenue
Maitland, FL 32751
(407) 539-0990

Manatees are large, slow, air-breathing mammals that eat 60 to 100 pounds of aquatic plants a day, plants that would otherwise clog Florida's waterways. While once plentiful, there are now as few as 1,200 manatees remaining in the U.S. This small population is continually threatened today by careless boaters, canal locks, barges, crab traps, and fishing lines. Founded in 1981 by a former governor of Florida, Bob Graham, and singer/songwriter Jimmy Buffett, the Save the Manatee Club cleverly offers a manatee adoption along with each membership in the club. Twenty-four manatees that regularly winter at Blue Spring State Park near Orange City, FL, are the official "adoptees"; each has a known history and in some cases has been tracked by radio-telemetry by U.S. Fish & Wildlife Service researchers. Membership is only $15 ($25 for a family); each member will be provided with an adoption certificate, photo of his or her shared manatee, and a biography of that animal.

WhaleWatch
International Wildlife Coalition
320 Gifford Street
Falmouth, MA 02540
(508) 564-9980

For $15 a year, WhaleWatch will enable you to adopt a whale. You'll receive a picture of your whale, a certificate with your whale's name on it, a migration map with information about where your whale has been sighted, a calendar, plus a quarterly newsletter.

GIFTS AND MERCHANDISE:
Helping to Support Animal Rights Organizations and Causes

Fundraising is a constant problem for all animal rights and humane groups, and many have chosen to create T-shirts and sweatshirts, bumper stickers, buttons, and a variety of other merchandise to sell to raise funds. These make excellent gifts for friends who care about animals—and they're fun to order for yourself, too. In addition to the merchandise mentioned below (with prices and order numbers specified, so that you can order right from these pages), there are usually additional goods offered by each, including books and pamphlets. And, of course, more groups than the few listed below offer T-shirts and additional merchandise; this is a representative sampling. Most of those listed accept payment by check or money order only; the few who accept payment via credit card are indicated.

Animal Liberation Front
Support Group of America (ALFSG)
P.O. Box 3623
San Bernardino, CA 92413

The purpose of the ALFSG is to support the Animal Liberation Front (yes, they're the ones who break into laboratories and liberate animals and incriminating data)—without breaking the law. Here's a way you can support direct action and get really extraordinary merchandise at the same time. The official ALFSG "logo" (a graphically sophisticated masked liberator holding a just-freed beagle) appears on several items: a coffee mug (#801—$6 + $1.50 shipping); a T-shirt (S, M, L, XL, white/blue/gray, $14 + $1 shipping); a sweatshirt; decal; notecards. They also have a number of "Liberation T-shirts and sweatshirts," each with a different design commemorating a particular raid: the Univ. of California/Riverside, for example, shows a masked liberator holding a baby monkey; the Univ. of Oregon depicts a liberator holding a cat; Loma Linda shows a liberator with a just-freed dog. These are great shirts. ALFSG also offers quite an interesting set of Christmas cards: the illustration on the cover is of a group of masked ALF members with rescued animals; the message inside reads, "Peace and Liberation" (No. 202, $16 for 25 + $1.50 shipping).

The Alaska Wildlife Alliance
P.O. Box 202022
Anchorage, AK 99520

If you're interested in the plight of wolves, you'll like the T-shirts, and crewneck and hooded sweatshirts offered by the Alaska Wildlife Alliance. These show a marvelous illustration of a wolf, full face, plus a smaller illustration of a baying wolf. The two are placed just beneath the words, "The Wolf. The Spirit of Alaska." The T-shirt comes in eleven colors: burgundy, powder blue, red, light blue, aqua, silver, lavender, turquoise, pink, white, yellow, $11 ppd. Crewneck sweatshirts come in red, heather gray, island blue, and raspberry, $20 ppd. Hooded sweatshirts with handwarmer pockets come in red, gray, blue, or pink, $25 ppd. All are in S, M, L, XL. They ask that you state a second color choice. They also have terrific enameled cloisonné pins: "Stop the Wolf Hunt," "Bears of Alaska," and "Keep Them Free" orca (killer whale). The wolf pin shows a wolf fleeing from an airplane. These sell for $10 each, ppd. Other pins depict the bald eagle, walrus, bull moose, orca, humpback whale.

Alliance for Animals
P.O. Box 909
Boston, MA 02103

Alliance for Animals offers a Fur Fighters Action Kit. This consists of: a 3″ button with the face of an appealing raccoon and the legend "Fur, The Look That Kills"; a "Fur, The Look That Kills" bumper sticker; a window decal; 25 stamps and 10 color leaflets. $5 + $2 shipping.

Animal Rights Mobilization

P.O. Box 1553
Williamsport, PA 17703

Animal Rights Mobilization has some excellent T-shirts ($10) and sweat-shirts ($18). One, in black or white, shows a puppy behind bars, with the legend "Animal Research. Taxes for Torture." Another, in T-shirt version only, shows two pigs nuzzling each other and says "Liberate Farm Animals. Go Vegetarian." One of the most interesting shirts shows a wild cat on the front and says "Beauty. Don't Buy Fur"; the back shows an otherwise attractive woman in a fur coat and says, "Beast. Don't Buy Fur." All shirts are available in S, M, L, and XL. ARM! also has bumper stickers with legends like "Fur . . . The Ultimate Sadist Symbol" and "Warning! I Don't Brake for Vivisectors," each $1. Buttons range from "Fur Hurts" to "Beans Give Strength, Go Vegetarian." $1 each. Add 15% for shipping.

ASPCA

Special Offers
441 East 92 Street
New York, NY 10128

The ASPCA has T-shirts featuring an excellent graphic in black on white of Henry Bergh, "The Great Meddler"—founder of the ASPCA. $10 + shipping.

Earth Island Institute Dolphin Project

300 Broadway (Suite 28)
San Francisco, CA 94133
(415) 788-3666

Earth Island has full-color T-shirts screened with non-toxic ink onto white 100% cotton shirts (S, M, L; child's sizes S, M, L). These depict schools of dolphins swimming just beneath the surface of the sea (No. D200), or the Earth Island/Save It design (No. 1500). These cost $11 in adult size, $9 for children, + $2 postage and handling. They have excellent dolphin jewelry and dolphin-shaped bumper stickers.

Farm Sanctuary

P.O. Box 150
Watkins Glen, NY 14891
(607) 583-2225

Farm Sanctuary has some interesting, reasonably priced T-shirts. Item T1 (black and green on white; S, M, L, XL) says "If You Love Animals Called Pets . . . Why Do You Eat Animals Called Dinner?" $8. Another, item T2, shows farm animals climbing a rainbow toward a better world. This one says "Free Farm Animals." $8.50. Another T-shirt, Item T6, shows a good-looking graphic of a veal calf in a crate and says "Boycott Veal." The back has a "Recipe for Milk-Fed Veal" that will startle the uninformed; blue background, $9. A sweatshirt version of this design is available too, for $18.

International Society for Animal Rights
Merchandise Orders Dept.
421 South State Street
Clarks Summit, PA 18411
(717) 586-2200   *(VISA and MasterCard accepted)*

ISAR offers T-shirts and sweatshirts bearing the statement: FUR COATS are worn by BEAUTIFUL ANIMALS and UGLY PEOPLE. These are available in black with white lettering, and in white with black lettering. T-shirts come in M, L, XL, sweatshirts in L and XL. $25 postpaid. These make one look rather like a walking billboard, but better a walking billboard than a barbarian swathed in dead animals. By the way, ISAR's NYC thrift shop, Return Engagement, can use donations of fine china, crystal, bric-a-brac, jewelry, and designer clothing. For more information, contact: Barbara Winkelman, Return Engagement, 900 First Avenue, NY, NY 10022, (212) 752-2679.

Feminists for Animal Rights
P.O. Box 10017
North Berkeley Station
Berkeley, CA 94709

Feminists for Animal Rights has some excellent logo T-shirts, with a stylized, curled up-fox in the center and the name of the organization wrapped in a circle around it. The color combinations are superb: turquoise on pink; black on Kelly green; black on fuchsia; white on black; pink on gray. Each comes in S, M, L, XL; $10 + $1 shipping. They also have a distinctive rubber stamp, showing a frazzled monkey with a laboratory torture device around its head. The legend reads, "No More Torture. Stop Animal Experimentation." $3.50. There's an interesting cookbook offered too: *The Second Seasonal Political Palate* ($10.95 + $1 shipping), a feminist vegetarian cookbook.

Friends of Animals
P.O. Box 1244
Norwalk, CT 06856
(MasterCard and VISA accepted for orders over $15)

Friends of Animals has some distinctive T-shirts and sweatshirts, a couple of which come in children's sizes. Its T-shirt shows an eagle with folded wings, with the words "Extinct Is Forever" above it, the name of the organization below. Blue only. Men's S, M, L, XL, $8. A gold-colored T-shirt carries a very nice illustration of a stalking tiger, with the same legend. Their sweatshirt, printed in shades of brown on white, shows an almost-too-cute puppy and kitten snuggling against each other, above the words, "Friends of Animals." S, M, L only, $15. For children, you can get a wonderful black and white illustration of a panda, printed on red, with the "Extinct Is Forever" legend above it, or a tortoise, printed on green. These come in S (6–8), M (10–12), or L (14–16); $8. Friends of Animals also has a variety of buttons, key rings, and bumper stickers, including one that says, "Support the Right to Arm Bears."

The Fund for Animals
18740 Highland Valley Road
Ramona, CA 92065

As this book goes to press, The Fund for Animals is in the process of getting new merchandise, so send for its current catalog. In the past it has had "Support Your Right to Arm Bears" T-shirts, mugs, books, notecards, and regulation-size "POSTED" signs.

People for the Ethical Treatment of Animals
PETA Merchandise
P.O. Box 42516
Washington, DC 20015-0516
(800) 673-8501   *(MasterCard and VISA accepted)*

PETA has a wide variety of merchandise that may interest you. They carry a few Allen's Naturally products and a few cosmetics and toiletries, but they also have a number of other items, ranging from sweatshirts and T-shirts, to ceramic mugs, an apron, vinyl-strap watch, buttons, postcards, and more. The classic PETA sweatshirt is black, with an extremely effective graphic of a caged primate printed in white. The legend is the name of the organization and the address. This distinctive sweatshirt is also available in white, printed in black (No. 1-310; S, M, L, XL; $15 for non-members, $13.50 for members). A T-shirt with this design is available for $12 ($10.75 for members). PETA also has a Fur Is Dead T-shirt, printed in black and red on white; same sizes and prices as above. For children, they have a peaceful rabbit T-shirt, showing a bunny sitting on a hill or mountaintop, looking off into the evening sky (No. 1-704, S, M, L), for $8 ($7.25 for PETA members). The same design is available for adults, $18 for the sweatshirt version ($16.25 for members,), $15 for the T-shirt ($13.50 for members).

Rainforest Alliance
295 Madison Avenue (Suite 1804)
New York, NY 10017
(212) 599-5060

The Rainforest Alliance has a couple of excellent T-shirts. The very colorful, silkscreened, "Save the Rainforest" T-shirt is designed by Raul del Rio, and comes in Macaw or Jungle of Birds designs. Adults' S, M, L, XL cost $11; XXL sells for $12. A long-sleeved Jungle of Birds design shirt, in L or XL, sells for $14. The children's Jungle of Birds, S, M, L, costs $8. They also have a "Save the Coral Reefs" T-shirt, designed by Raul del Rio, for $11 (XXL costs $12). A version of this one for children is available for $8. The Rainforest Alliance has some other great gift items, too. These include posters, notecards, buttons, bumper stickers, calendars.

United Action for Animals
205 East 42 Street
New York, NY 10017
(212) 983-5315

The thrust of United Action for Animals is companion animal overpopulation, so one T-shirt shows a winsome kitten, the other a puppy. Above each is the legend "Share the Responsibility," beneath is the name of the organization. Frankly, these T-shirts would make more sense if they said, "Help End Overpopulation, Spay Your Cat or Dog." But the shirts are cute. White only, with choice of black, red, or blue lettering, S, M, L, XL. $15. Another shirt simply has the initials of the organization as a bold graphic and above, "United Action for Animals."

VACATIONS HELPING ANIMALS:
How to Do Good While Having Fun

How you spend your vacation time is as personal a decision as the way you spend your money. All we can say is that one animal-loving friend, who had already traveled literally around the world, including a photographic safari to Kenya, came back from an Earthwatch trip to San Juan Island, Washington, last summer—a trip during which she and other volunteers worked to help unravel the family dynamics of the killer whale—with the comment, "It was the best vacation of my life." This year she's going to work with musk oxen.

The pleasant surprise is that several of the trips that follow are tax-deductible (consult the trip providers, as well as your own accountant).

Cetacean Society International
P.O. Box 9145
Wethersfield, CT 06109

In cooperation with the Center for Studies of Whales and Dolphins, Göteborg, Sweden, the Cetacean Society is distributing information in the United States about an interesting but very brief whale-watching/research trip. As visitors to Andoya, Norway, participants become involved in the work carried out by whale scientists, essentially by financing the research crews' trips out to the whale feeding area. Trips are held, believe it or not, on a whale boat, the *Kromhaut*—one that still carries cannon and crow's nest. This is really "ecotourism": a trip that helps the local population substitute income from tourism for income from killing off a natural resource. While worthwhile, this is one of the least "hands-on" trips listed here. In the past, the Cetacean Society has been involved in other, more volunteer-intensive vacations: the Benign Whale Research Project, for example, in 1989, and a dolphin project off the Bahamas that same year.

Community of Compassion for Animals
c/o 5005 Sleepy Hollow Lane
Suisun, CA 94585

This sanctuary for former farm and laboratory animals needs volunteers. Write to them if you have a block of time available.

Earthwatch
680 Mount Auburn Street
Box 403
Watertown, MA 02272

This is one of the most exciting programs available to people who care about animals. It provides a chance for volunteers to work alongside eminent scientists on important research projects around the world. People who participate one year seem to go right back again the next. The volunteer possibilities are astounding—and your participation really makes a difference. At the time of this writing, for example, volunteers were scheduled to go to Vietnam, to work in the Tram Chim wetland area, which was devastated during the war. Along with Dr. George Archibald and his colleague

Le Dien Duc, participants were needed to help develop a management plan to save the Eastern Saurus cranes, the tallest flying birds in the world. Volunteers were scheduled to live in dormitories in Tam Nong, and to travel early each morning by boat to the dikes and blinds within Tram Chim. There, pairs of volunteers were to use telescopes to help document the crane's feeding behavior, as well as their time budgets in different habitats.

But you don't necessarily have to go to Vietnam to do good work. Earthwatch sends teams to the forests of Michigan to study the diet, reproduction, and behavior of the bald eagle. Teams of volunteers have gone to the Sea of Cortez to determine how development and whales can co-exist. From April to July, volunteers are needed around the clock in St. Croix, U.S. Virgin Islands, to monitor the nesting and hatching of endangered leatherback turtles. Or you can work with: baboons along Ethiopia's Awash River; black bears in North Carolina; track timber wolves in Minnesota; study kangaroos in New South Wales, Australia; or go to Alaska to work with non-migratory musk oxen.

Farm Sanctuary
P.O. Box 150
Watkins Glen, NY 14891
(607) 583-2225

Farm Sanctuary is one of only two shelters in the country for animals who have suffered the abuses and deprivation of factory farms, stockyards, and slaughterhouses. They presently have two facilities, one near Avondale, PA, and the other in Watkins Glen, NY. Positions are all filled by volunteers, and range from office work or animal feeding and care, to hay farming, barn maintenance, or conducting education tours. Interested animal activists can apply for their Sanctuary Internship Program, which requires a 40-hour, five-day-a-week commitment and can last from two to three months. Unlike most of the other programs listed here, Farm Sanctuary actually pays volunteers; they provide accommodations and a whopping $25 a week food allowance. This is a very good organization.

Foundation for Field Research
P.O. Box 2010
Alpine, CA 92001
(619) 445-9264

The Foundation for Field Research is a nonprofit organization founded to coordinate a variety of research expeditions. Volunteers act as field assistants, actively participating in work being done by accomplished ornithologists, paleontologists, primatologists, and others. As with Earthwatch, volunteers pay a share-of-cost contribution that covers meals, lodging, and ground transportation and provides for the researchers' expenses as well, including equipment and supplies. Lengths of stay on Foundation trips vary from a couple of days to one month. At the time of this writing, volunteer opportunities include: helping in a study of tool use among chimpanzees in Liberia, West Africa; traveling to Corsica, France, to observe female fidelity in a unique fish called the ocellated wrasse; accumulating data on the endangered sea turtles of Grenada, West Indies; evaluating population parameters and vegetation characteristics of two colonies of prairie dogs in Montana; and studying the impact of whale-watching vessels on migrating whales in the St. Lawrence Seaway, Canada.

The Marin County Humane Society
171 Bel Marin Keys Boulevard
Novato, CA 94949

This is a slightly different type of program, as it's exclusively for children. It's basically a day camp, with two-week sessions for young people aged 12–15, and one-week sessions for children 9–11; but it sets up an opportunity for children to get involved in animal rights issues independent of their parents.

Natural Habitat Wildlife Adventures
Route 171 North (Box 789)
McAfee, NJ 07428

Natural Habitat coordinates a fascinating trip for the International Fund for Animal Welfare, which was founded in 1969 to end the Canadian and Norwegian Harp and hood seal hunts. Each year now (the trip is relatively new), more and more people are signing up to travel to the Magdalen Islands, for what has become an annual Seal Watch trip. While this is not the sort of volunteer/research project offered by Earthwatch and the Foundation for Field Research, this is still an extremely worthwhile trip, for a variety of reasons. First, it was set up to bring tourists to a remote destination, where previously one of the few viable means of support was hunting; these trips are proving to the local population that the seals are worth more alive than dead. Second, as well as increasing the knowledge of participants, the trips are simply great fun. The Seal Watch staff offer a variety of presentations and workshops on seals, wildlife, and photography. They also provide transportation by helicopter to the ice floes, where participants witness the epic annual seal migration and have a chance to come close to the appealing little white-furred Harp seals.

NOW IS THE TIME TO JOIN:
A Guide to Animal Rights Organizations

Organizations Mentioned Throughout This Book

The brief or telegraphic descriptions following most entries indicate the aspect of the group's work mentioned in the preceding pages; some organizations have a much wider sphere of concerns than that indicated. If an organization's name is self-explanatory, no description follows.

Action 81, Inc.
Route 3 (Box 6000)
Berryville, VA 22611
(703) 955-1278
(Pet theft)

Actors and Others for Animals
5510 Cahuenga Boulevard
North Hollywood, CA 91601
(818) 985-6263

African Wildlife Foundation
1717 Massachusetts Avenue, NW
Washington, DC 20036
(202) 265-8394

Alaska Wildlife Alliance
P.O. Box 202022
Anchorage, AK 99520
(907) 227-0897
(Emphasis on ending wolf and polar bear hunts. Broader concerns as well.)

Alliance for Animals
P.O. Box 909
Boston, MA 02103
(Fur, plus broader concerns.)

American Anti-Vivisection Society
Suite 204—Noble Plaza
801 Old York Road
Jenkintown, PA 19046-1685
(Laboratory experimentation, factory farming, more. Educational materials available.)

American Society for the Prevention of Cruelty to Animals
441 East 92 Street
New York, NY 10128
(Animal rescue, veterinary services, issue management, educational materials.)

Animal Aid
1423 South Harvard
Tulsa, OK 74112
(Companion animals.)

Animal Legal Defense Fund
1363 Lincoln Avenue
San Rafael, CA 94901
(Classroom dissection and other issues. They're looking for more volunteer attorneys.)

Animal Liberation Front Support Group of America
P.O. Box 3623
San Bernardino, CA 92413
(The ALF itself {not the support group} has been listed by the FBI as a terrorist organization. Many people in the animal rights movement consider the ALF heroes.)

Animal Protection Institute
P.O. Box 22502
Sacramento, CA 95822
(916) 422-1921
(They point out that they're "an animal welfare organization, not an animal rights organization.")

Animal Rights International
P.O. Box 214
Planetarium Station
New York, NY 10024
(Factory farming plus other issues. See Preface.)

Animal Rights Mobilization
(formerly Trans-Species Unlimited)
P.O. Box 1553
Williamsport, PA 17703
(717) 322-3252
New York: (212) 966-8490
Chicago: (312) 751-0118
(Fur, laboratory experimentation, plus other issues. Direct action-oriented, with grass roots network. Publications, educational materials available. Vegan-run.)

Ark II
P.O. Box 11049
Washington, DC 20008
(301) 897-5429

Ark II
542 Mount Pleasant Road (Suite 104)
Toronto, Ontario M4S 2M7
Canada
(416) 487-4681
(Sponsoring Gillette boycott.)

**Association of
  Veterinarians for
  Animal Rights**
15 Dutch Street (Suite 500A)
New York, NY 10038-3779
(212) 962-7055

Canadian Anti-Fur Alliance
Toronto Humane Society
11 River Street
Toronto, Ontario M5A 4C2
Canada

Cetacean Society International
P.O. Box 9145
Wethersfield, CT 06109
(Whales, dolphins.)

**Coalition for
  Pet Population Control**
1053 Colorado Boulevard (Suite G)
Los Angeles, CA 90041
(213) 256-0000
(Low cost spay/neuter hotline.)

Earth Island Institute
300 Broadway (Suite 28)
San Francisco, CA 94133
(415) 788-3666
(Dolphins.)

Farm Animal Reform Movement
10101 Ashburton Lane
Bethesda, MD 20817

Farm Sanctuary
Box 37
Rockland, DE 19732

Feminists for Animal Rights
P.O. Box 10017
North Berkeley Station
Berkeley, CA 94709

Food Animals Concerns Trust
P.O. Box 14599
Chicago, IL 60614
(312) 525-4952

Friends of Animals
P.O. Box 1244
Norwalk, CT 06856
(Companion animals, fur, spay/neuter hotline.)

Fund for Animals
200 West 57 Street
New York, NY 10019
(212) 246-2096
(212) 246-2632
(Cleveland Amory's group. Companion animals, fur, abuse of animals in entertainment, more. Runs three sanctuaries.)

Greenpeace
1436 U Street NW
Washington, DC 20009
(Whales, dolphins.)

Greyhound Friends, Inc.
167 Saddle Hill Road
Hopkinton, MA 01748
(Retired racing greyhound adoptions.)

Greyhound Pets of America
c/o Millie Merritt
750 Willard Street
Quincy, MA 02169
(617) 472-4055
(Retired racing greyhound adoptions.)

Humane Farming Association
1550 California Street, #6
San Francisco, CA 94109

**Humane Society
  of the United States**
2100 L Street, NW
Washington, DC 20037
(Covers all animals' issues, but some broader concerns as well {i.e., National Refuge System, and environmental issues}. Extensive range of publications.)

**Illinois Citizens
  for Humane Legislation**
2520 North Lincoln Avenue (Box 170)
Chicago, IL 60614
(312) 288-3838
(Stop the Draize test in Illinois.)

**International Fund for
  Animal Welfare**
P.O. Box 193
Yarmouth Port, MA 02675
(617) 362-4944

**International Society
  for Animal Rights**
421 South State Street
Clarks Summit, PA 18411
(717) 586-2200
(Fur, plus broad range of concerns. Educational materials available.)

**International
  Wildlife Coalition**
P.O. Box 388
North Falmouth, MA 02556
(508) 540-8086

**International
  Wildlife Coalition—Canada**
P.O. Box 461
Port Credit Postal Station
Mississauga, Ontario L5G 4MI
Canada
(Fur.)

Last Chance for Animals
18653 Ventura Boulevard, #356
Tarzana, CA 91356
(818) 760-2075
HOTLINE. (818) 760-8340

Marin County Humane Society
171 Bel Marin Keys Boulevard
Novato, CA 94949
(415) 883-3522

**Medical Research
  Modernization Committee**
P.O. Box 6036
Grand Central Station
New York, NY 10163-6018
(212) 876-1368

Michigan Humane Society
7401 Chrysler Drive
Detroit, MI 48211
(313) 872-3400

**National Alliance
for Animal Legislation**
P.O. Box 75116
Washington, DC 20013-5116
(703) 684-0654

**National Association for the
Advancement of Humane
and Environmental Education**
67 Salem Road
East Haddam, CT 06423
(Humane teaching materials.)

**National Association
of Biology Teachers**
c/o Rosaline Hairston
11250 Roger Bacon Drive, #19
Reston, VA 22090
(Alternatives to dissection.)

**Network for
Ohio Animal Action**
P.O. Box 21004
Cleveland, OH 44121
(216) 321-6222

**New Jersey
Animal Rights Alliance**
P.O. Box 703
Woodbridge, NJ 07095
(201) 855-9092
*(Stop the Draize in NJ. Locally grounded group with
national concerns.)*

**New York City
Central Board of Education
Humane Education Committee**
P.O. Box 445
New York, NY 10028
(212) 410-3095

**Ohio Humane Education
Association**
P.O. Box 546
Grove City, OH 43146

**People for the Ethical
Treatment of Animals**
Box 42516
Washington, DC 20015
(301) 770-7444
*(National group with no local chapters {Ask and
they'll provide you with the name of an animal rights
group near where you live}. Publications and educational materials available. Vegan-run.)*

**Physicians Committee
for Responsible Medicine**
P.O. Box 6322
Washington, DC 20015
(202) 686-2210

**Psychologists for the
Ethical Treatment of Animals**
P.O. Box 87
New Gloucester, ME 04260
(207) 926-4817

Rainforest Alliance
295 Madison Avenue (Suite 1804)
New York, NY 10017
(212) 599-5060

Reptile Defense Fund
5025 Julane Dr.
Baton Rouge, LA 70808

**Sea Shepherd Conservation
Society**
P.O. Box 7000
Redondo Beach, CA 90277
(Whales.)

Stop Taking Our Pets
Box 1032
Solana Beach, CA 92075
(Pound seizure.)

**Student Action Corps
for Animals**
P.O. Box 15588
Washington, DC 15588
(202) 543-8983
(Contact them to find a local group.)

United Action for Animals
205 East 42 Street
New York, NY 10017
(212) 983-5315
(Companion animals.)

Wildlife Refuge Reform Coalition
P.O. Box 18414
Washington, DC 20036
(202) 778-6145

Other Worthwhile Animal Rights Organizations

This list is by no means complete. The fact that a group is not included is in no way meant to impugn their contribution to the cause of animal rights.

Individuals or groups who would like a more comprehensive listing should contact: Animal Rights Information & Education Service, Inc., P.O. Box 332, Rowayton, CT 06853, (203) 866-0523. Aries has, over the past two years, compiled a guide to 850 animal rights organizations. The *Aries Group List* sells for $10.

American Horse Protection Association
1000 29 Street NW
Washington, DC 20007
(202) 965-0500

Animal Defense & Anti-Vivisection Society of British Columbia
P.O. Box 391
Postal Station A
Vancouver, BC
Canada V6C 2N2
(604) 733-3486

Canadians Against Fur
Box 198
Station G
Toronto, Ontario
Canada M4M 3G7

Center for Marine Conservation
1725 DeSales Street, NW
Washington, DC 20036
(202) 429-5609

Committee to Abolish Sport Hunting
P.O. Box 43
White Plains, NY 10605

Disabled Against Animal Research & Experimentation
1836 Carroll Avenue
St. Paul, MN 55104

Disabled and Incurably Ill for Alternatives to Animal Research
1636 Channing Way
Berkeley, CA 94703

Doris Day Animal League
111 Massachusetts Avenue, NW
Washington, DC 20001-1461

Fund for the Replacement of Animals in Medical Education (FRAME)
Eastgate House
34 Stoney Street
Nottingham NG1 1NB
England

International Association Against Painful Experiments on Animals

175 West 12 Street
New York, NY 10011

Legal Action for Animals

205 East 42 Street
New York, NY 10017
(212) 818-0130

(This is the place to turn if your landlord is trying to evict you because of your companion animals. They'll also help with veterinary malpractice situations, defense of civil disobedience on behalf of animals, and more.)

Lifeforce

Box 3117, Main Post Office
Vancouver, BC V6B 3X6
Canada

Massachusetts Society for the Prevention of Cruelty to Animals

350 South Huntington Avenue
Boston, MA 02130
(617) 522-7400

(Vet hospital: spay-neuter: shelters, issues-oriented legislation and education.)

National Anti-Vivisection Society

53 W. Jackson Boulevard
(Suite 1550)
Chicago, IL 60604
(312) 427-6065

National Association of Nurses Against Vivisection

P.O. Box 42110
Washington, DC 20015
(301) 770-8961

Primarily Primates

P.O. Box 15306
San Antonio, TX 78212-8506
(512) 755-4616

(Sanctuary for unwanted or abused exotic animals, but primarily primates.)

Society for the Protection of Endangered Turtles

c/o Jeff Wright
1717 West Fourth Street
Wilmington, DE 19805
(302) 571-1718

Students United to Protest Research on Sentient Subjects (SUPRESS)

740 East Colorado Boulevard
(Suite 205)
Pasadena, CA 91101
(818) 798-3300

Toronto Humane Society

11 River Street
Toronto, Ontario
Canada M5A 4C2

Wisconsin Horse and Pony Humane Society

N88 West 22937 North Lisbon Road
Sussex, WI 53089

SUGGESTED READING

Periodicals

Most of the organizations listed on the preceding pages publish their own newsletters or magazines. You'll receive them along with your membership. In addition, you may be interested in subscribing to one or more of the following.

Alternatives to Animals Newsletter

P.O. Box 7177
San Jose, CA 95150
(408) 996-1405

Quarterly. $15. Newsletter on alternatives to testing and experimentation on animals. Primarily from biomedical and behavioral journals.

Animals' Agenda

P.O. Box 6809
Syracuse, NY 13217
(800) 825-0061

Monthly. $22 per year. News, articles. Almost always has animal rights news you won't find in the newspaper.

Animal Network Calendar of Events

Maureen Koplow
476 Warwick Road
Deptford, NJ 06096
(609) 853-1847

Monthly. $15. Newsletter packed with information on upcoming animal rights events primarily in the PA, NJ, and (to a lesser degree) NY area.

The Animals' Voice Magazine

P.O. Box 16955
North Hollywood, CA 91615

Bi-monthly. $18 per year. News, articles. Extremely worthwhile new magazine.

The Aries Newsletter

Animal Rights Information
& Education Service, Inc.
P.O. Box 332
Rowayton, CT 06853

Monthly. $12 a year. Densely-packed newsletter with information on animal rights issues and events.

KIND News, Jr.

67 Salem Road
East Haddam, CT 06423-0362
(203) 434-8666

Bi-monthly. $20, in packets of 30 for classroom use. Probably best for second and third graders. Lots of involvement devices.

Movement Mag

Animal Rights Mobilization (ARM!)
P.O. Box 1553
Williamsport, PA 17703
(717) 322-3252
(800) CALL ARM

New grassroots magazine scheduled to debut in late summer 1990. Call for more information.

PETA Kids
P.O. Box 42516
Washington, DC 20015-0516
(301) 770-7444
Quarterly. $3. Animal rights news and games for children. Quick stories about what other children are doing to help animals. Children about 8 and up.

Wolves and Related Canids
P.O. Box 1026
Agoura, CA 91301
50-page magazine on wolves, with some attention paid to foxes, coyotes. $25 year.

Books

The following list is at best perfunctory. The fact that any book or publication in the growing body of animal rights literature is not included is not in any way meant to denigrate its importance.

Where a publication can be ordered directly from its publisher, an address is given. If your local bookstore does not have a book you want, ask them to order it for you.

A single asterisk (*) indicates that a publication can be ordered from People for the Ethical Treatment of Animals, Merchandise Dept., P.O. Box 42516, Washington, DC 20015-0516. Credit card purchases: (800) 673-8501. Shipping charges: Less than a $10 purchase, $3; $10 to $20, $4; more than $20, $5. Second day UPS available at extra charge. A double asterisk (**) indicates that it can be ordered from *The Animals' Voice Magazine*, P.O. Box 341347, Los Angeles, CA 90034. Credit card ordering: (800) 82-VOICE. Shipping charges: for 1 to 3 books, add $2; for 4 or more books, add $3. CA residents must add 6% sales tax; 6½% in Los Angeles.

Animal Factories, by Jim Mason and Peter Singer (Crown, 1980). An important exposé of modern factory farming methods. An eye-opening book. $9.95 plus postage.*

Animal Liberation, by Peter Singer (New York Review, 1975, 1990). Considered the "Bible" of the animal rights movement. The first chapter is dense reading, but do persist; this is an important, fascinating book that defines the basic ethical issues of animal rights. $3.95 plus postage.* **

The Case for Animal Rights, by Tom Regan (University of California Press, 1983). With Peter Singer's *Animal Liberation,* the ethical backbone of the animal rights movement. Scholarly, interesting. $9.95 plus postage.**

A Critical Look at Animal Research (Medical Research Modernization Committee, P.O. Box 6036, Grand Central Station, New York, NY 10163-6018). A well-written, accessible, well-documented overview of the problems with many types of animal research. Booklet. Free on request to students, journalists, health care professionals.

Cruel Deception: The Use of Animals in Medical Research, by Dr. Robert Sharpe (Thorsons Publishers Ltd., 1988). Fascinating and upsetting discussion of this highly-charged issue. Strong indictment of AIDs research on endangered chimpanzees, and good discussion of the importance of antivivisection in schools. $13 plus postage.*

Diet for a New America, by John Robbins (Stillpoint Publishing, Box 640, Walpole, NH 03608, (800) 847-4014). Frightening information about depletion of natural resources to provide a meat-based diet, plus additional information on factory farming, and antibiotics and pesticides in meat. $10.95.**

Diet for a Small Planet, by Frances Moore Lappé (Ballantine Books, 1982). Look for the revised and updated edition. The vegetarian how-to-do-it that sold more than 2 million copies. The updated version places less emphasis on food combinations. Look in the cookbook section of your bookstore.

Dogs and Cats Go Vegetarian, by Barbara Lynn Peden (Hart-Binger House, P.O. Box 146, Swisshome, OR 97480). $9.95 plus postage. Not all veterinarians agree that dogs can live healthfully even on a supplemented vegetarian diet, but there are certainly dogs who have done well on this regime. Cats going vegetarian is even more controversial.*

The Endangered Species Handbook, by Greta Nilsson (Animal Welfare Institute, P.O. Box 3650, Washington, DC 20007). $6 plus postage. Meant as a classroom test providing humane science projects, this is in fact an awfully good, extremely interesting introductory text on endangered species, well suited to a general reader.

Haggadah for the Liberated Lamb (Micah Publications, 255 Humphrey Street, Marblehead, MA 01945). Vegetarian seder Haggadah. Hebrew/English paperback, $14.95; cloth, $24.95. Enclose $1.40 postage.

In Defense of Animals, edited by Peter Singer (Perennial Library, 1985). Anthology of some of the most interesting and pivotal thinking on animal rights issues, from zoos, to the doomed Silver Springs monkeys, to factory farming. $5.50 plus postage.*

Legislative Summary (National Alliance for Animal Legislation, P.O. Box 75116, Washington, DC 20013, (703) 684-0654). The clearest, most accessible information on pending legislation pertaining to animals and animal rights. Free on request.

Living Without Cruelty, by Mark Gold (Green Print, 1988). Excellent, pragmatic look at how one can live a kinder, more compassionate life. Includes vegetarian recipes by Sarah Brown. A British book; if you can't find it here, ask a friend to bring it back from England.

Nontoxic & Natural: A Guide for Consumers, by Debra Lynn Dadd (Jeremy P. Tarcher, Inc., 1984). Available from: The Earthwise Consumer, P.O. Box 1506, Mill Valley, CA 94942. $9.95 + $2 shipping. How to avoid dangerous everyday products and buy or make safe ones. Lots of mail order sources, many do-it-yourself formulas.

Shopping for a Better World: A Quick & Easy Guide to Socially Responsible Supermarket Shopping (Council on Economic Priorities, 30 Irving Place, New York, NY 10003, (800) 822-6435). $5.95. From cough syrup to fuel oil, who tests on animals, who's discriminating against women, who's polluting the environment.

Slaughter of the Innocent, by Hans Ruesch (Civitas, 1985). Animal abuse in laboratory experimentation. A classic, shocking, antivivisectionist text attacking animal use in medical experimentation as fraud. $3.95 plus postage.***

Tell It to Washington: A Guide for Citizen Action (League of Women Voters Education Fund, 1730 M Street NW, Washington, DC 20038). How to most effectively communicate with elected and appointed government officials, including their addresses. $2 plus postage.